KT-213-177

Series / Number 07-049

BASIC CONTENT ANALYSIS
SECOND EDITION

ROBERT PHILIP WEBER
Harvard University

SAGE PUBLICATIONS
The International Professional Publishers
Newbury Park   London   New Delhi

Copyright © 1990 by Sage Publications, Inc.

All rights reserved. No part of this book may be reproduced or utilized in any form or by any means, electronic or mechanical, including photocopying, recording, or by any information storage and retrieval system, without permission in writing from the publisher.

For information address:

SAGE Publications, Inc.
2455 Teller Road
Newbury Park, California 91320
E-mail: order@sagepub.com

SAGE Publications Ltd.
6 Bonhill Street
London EC2A 4PU
United Kingdom

SAGE Publications India Pvt. Ltd.
M-32 Market
Greater Kailash I
New Delhi 110 048 India

Printed in the United States of America

International Standard Book Number 0-8039-3863-2

Library of Congress Catalog Card No. 90-061019

97 98 99 00 01 02 03 12 11 10 9 8 7 6

Sage Production Editor: Susan McElroy

When citing a University Paper, please use the proper form. Remember to cite the Sage University Paper series title and include the paper number. One of the following formats can be adapted (depending on the style manual used):

(1) HENKEL, RAMON E. (1976) Tests of Significance. Sage University Paper Series on Quantitative Applications in the Social Sciences, 07-004. Newbury Park, CA: Sage

OR

(2) Henkel, R. E. (1976) *Tests of significance* (Sage University Paper Series on Quantitative Applications in the Social Sciences, series no. 07-004). Newbury Park, CA: Sage.

CONTENTS

SERIES EDITOR'S INTRODUCTION

Content analysis classifies textual material, reducing it to more relevant, manageable bits of data. Social scientists who must make sense of historical documents, newspaper stories, political speeches, open-ended interviews, diplomatic messages, psychological diaries, or official publications — to name a few — will find the technique indispensable. Take, as an example, political propaganda studies in the field of mass communications. Suppose Professor West wishes to examine the use of anti-Communism as a tool of political rhetoric in the speeches of American presidents. Therefore, he "content-analyzes" the annual State of the Union messages since 1948, counting the appearance of the word *Communism* in each.

This simple content analysis raises many questions. Is the word *Communism* a valid measure of the researcher's concept? Is it reliable? Should a broader code category (e.g., ANTI-COMMUNISM) be constructed, with any of a set of words (e.g., *Communism, Russia, Soviet threat*) counted? How does this quantitative indicator relate to foreign policy behavior? What about other themes in these messages?

Questions of this nature are treated in Dr. Weber's fine monograph, from the creation of a simple coding scheme to an elaborate computer-aided analysis of content. He makes his points with numerous well-chosen pieces of text: U.S. political party platforms, the 1886 address of the British King to parliament, speeches of the Kaiser, and Korean War editorials from American newspapers. Moreover, the utility of working by computer is spelled out. Once the text is computerized, say with an optical scanner, it is relatively easy to make a classification from more than one dictionary. Moreover, with computers, the coding rules are necessarily made explicit, allowing for perfect "intercoder reliability." Also, many of the computer options would be virtually impossible by hand, such as key-word-in-context (KWIC), which prints the context (the surrounding sentences) around each and every use of the selected keyword.

AUTHOR'S NOTE: *The first edition of this book was sponsored by the former series editors, Richard Niemi and John Sullivan.*

Conveniently, Dr. Weber includes an Appendix that considers different computer programs for the analysis of text. At the end of each chapter, he provides a good discussion of current literature. Hence, this second edition is fully up-to-date, in terms of substance and technology. Lest we forget, however, he sagely reminds us that content analysis is still "in part an art" (Chapter 3). Dr. Weber finishes with a sensitive discussion of the unresolved problems (in measurement, indication, representation, and interpretation) remaining for content analysis.

—Michael S. Lewis-Beck
Series Editor

ACKNOWLEDGMENTS

Acknowledgments for Second Edition

Much of the material discussed in Chapter 4 will be covered in greater depth in a much longer piece coauthored with Zvi Namenwirth (Weber and Namenwirth, in press); Namenwirth's contribution, comments, and suggestions are greatly appreciated. Connie Zuell, Peter Philip Mohler, and Philip J. Stone provided continued encouragement and support, for which I am grateful. Much of the editing and rewriting was done in the *Patisserie Francaise* near Harvard Square. Many thanks to Elie and Salwa Matta and to Alexis (Gigi) Andrews for good food and hospitality.

Acknowledgments for First Edition

This research was supported in part by ZUMA, the Center for Surveys, Methods, and Analysis, Mannheim, FRG. I remain indebted to the generosity of past and present Directors and staff, especially, Hans-Dieter Klingemann, Peter Philip Mohler, Karl Ulrich Mayer, Max Kaase, and Manfred Keuchler. Additional support was provided by Kurzweil Computer products, Inc., a subsidiary of Xerox Corp. Sue Williamson of Kurzweil played a key role, and her generosity and help is gratefully acknowledged. Randi Lynn Miller assisted with data entry at an earlier phase of the research. Thanks to Nancy Marshall, J. Zvi Namenwirth, Barbara Norman, Philip J. Stone, Kathrine Tenerowicz, and two anonymous reviewers for detailed comments on earlier drafts. Thanks also to the Harvard University Computing Center for computer resources.

Thanks to Zvi Namenwirth for permission to quote extensively from Namenwirth and Bibbee (1975); to Dexter Dunphy for permission to reproduce a figure from Dunphy, Bullard, and Crossing (1974); to Human Sciences Press for permission to adapt or reprint some material from Weber (1984b); to Elsevier Publishing Company for permission to adapt or reprint some material from Weber (1983); and to the Austrian Academy of Sciences for permission to adapt or reprint some material that appeared in Weber (1984a).

BASIC CONTENT ANALYSIS
Second Edition

ROBERT PHILIP WEBER
Harvard University

1. INTRODUCTION

Content analysis is a research method that uses a set of procedures to make valid inferences from text.[1] These inferences are about the sender(s) of the message, the message itself, or the audience of the message. The rules of this inferential process vary with the theoretical and substantive interests of the investigator, and are discussed in later chapters.

Content analysis can be used for many purposes. The following list points out a few notable examples (adapted from Berelson, 1952):

- disclose international differences in communication content;
- compare media or "levels" of communication;
- audit communication content against objectives;
- code open-ended questions in surveys;
- identify the intentions and other characteristics of the communicator;
- determine the psychological state of persons or groups;
- detect the existence of propaganda;
- describe attitudinal and behavioral responses to communications;
- reflect cultural patterns of groups, institutions, or societies;
- reveal the focus of individual, group, institutional, or societal attention; and
- describe trends in communication content.

The numerous examples presented throughout this monograph mainly show the last three uses of content analysis.

This monograph is an introduction to content analysis methods from a social science perspective.[2] The material covered here will be useful to students and researchers who wish to analyze text. The following chapters assume that the reader has had at least introductory courses in research methods and in data analysis or social statistics.

Compared with other data-generating and analysis techniques, content analysis has several advantages:

- Communication is a central aspect of social interaction. Content-analytic procedures operate directly on text or transcripts of human communications.
- The best content-analytic studies use both qualitative and quantitative operations on texts. Thus content analysis methods combine what are usually thought to be antithetical modes of analysis.
- Documents of various kinds exist over long periods of time. Culture indicators generated from such series of documents constitute reliable data that may span even centuries (e.g., Namenwirth and Weber, 1987)
- In more recent times, when reliable data of other kinds exist, culture indicators can be used to assess quantitatively the relationships among economic, social, political, and cultural change.
- Compared with techniques such as interviews, content analysis usually yields unobtrusive measures in which neither the sender nor the receiver of the message is aware that it is being analyzed. Hence, there is little danger that the act of measurement itself will act as a force for change that confounds the data (Webb, Campbell, Schwartz, and Sechrist, 1981).

Two very different studies summarized below show some ways content analysis has been used. Following chapters explain other studies in greater detail.

Some Content-Analytic Studies

Content analysis has been used to study popular art forms. Walker (1975) analyzed differences and similarities in American black and white popular song lyrics, 1962-1973. Using computer-aided content analysis, Walker investigated differences in narrative form. He found that compared with popular white song lyrics, "rhythm and blues" and "soul" song lyrics showed greater emphasis on action in the objective world, less concern with time, and greater emphasis on what Walker calls "toughmindedness" or "existential concreteness."

The study also investigated changes in narrative focus. Walker found that identification with others increased significantly over time in "soul" and "rhythm and blues" lyrics, but not in popular white song lyrics. This change may reflect increasing self-awareness and positive images within the black community.

Walker's study illustrates that computer-based content analysis may be used to study popular and elite culture. In fact, one important substantive question content analysis might address is the relationship between popular and elite culture. Specifically, do changes in elite culture lead or lag behind changes in mass culture? Unfortunately, one serious difficulty exists in any study addressing this question. Textual materials that survive over long periods often reflect an elite bias.

In another study, Aries (1973; summarized in Aries, 1977), also using computer-aided content analysis, studied differences in female, male, and mixed-sex small groups. She found that differential sex-role socialization and sex-role stereotyping affect thematic content and social interaction. In female groups, women show much concern with interpersonal issues. Women discuss "themselves, their homes and families, and their relationships, defining themselves by the way they relate to the significant others who surround them" (Aries, 1973: 254).

In male groups, members do not address interpersonal matters directly. Instead, men indirectly relate personal experiences and feelings through stories and metaphors. Men "achieve a closeness through the sharing of laughter and stories of activities, rather than the sharing of the understanding of those experiences" (Aries, 1973: 254). Also, all-male groups manifest more themes involving aggression than do all-female groups.

In mixed groups, Aries found that women talked less of their homes and families. Women also spoke less of achievement and institutions. In short, women in these groups "orient themselves around being women with men by assuming the traditional female role" (Aries, 1973: 256). Men in mixed groups expressed their competitiveness less through storytelling than through assuming leadership roles in the group. Moreover, in the presence of women, men shift more toward reflection of themselves and their feelings.

Aries's study illustrates that content analysis may be:

- applied to substantive problems at the intersection of culture, social structure, and social interaction;
- used to generate dependent variables in experimental designs; and
- used to study small groups as microcosms of society.

Changes in sex-role socialization could be assessed by repeating the study. Furthermore, Aries's research could be extended with appropriate modifications to cross-national and cross-language research designs.

Issues in Content Analysis

A central idea in content analysis is that the many words of the text are classified into much fewer content categories. Each category may consist of one, several, or many words. Words, phrases, or other units of text classified in the same category are presumed to have similar meanings.[3] Depending on the purposes of the investigator, this similarity may be based on the precise meaning of the words (such as grouping synonyms together), or may be based on words sharing similar connotations (such as grouping together several words implying a concern with a concept such as WEALTH[4] or POWER). To make valid inferences from the text, it is important that the classification procedure be reliable in the sense of being consistent: Different people should code the same text in the same way. Also, the classification procedure must generate variables that are valid. A variable is valid to the extent that it measures or represents what the investigator intends it to measure. Because of their central importance, the second chapter discusses reliability, validity, and content classification in detail.

In the past, investigators have used a variety of methods to make inferences from text. The third chapter presents a wide range of techniques that have proved useful.[5] Some of the methods are quite simple and, in a sense, linguistically naive.[6] One should not make the mistake, however, of believing that naive procedures must be put to naive uses. Many of these simple techniques produce highly reliable and valid indicators of symbolic content. Other content-analytic techniques are more complex or are used with statistical methods. Chapter 3 explains the use of these techniques, but highly technical matters are handled by notes or references to the literature.

Because of the general proliferation of computers and the growing capacities for microcomputers, Chapter 3 focuses on computer-aided content analysis. Computers can be used to manipulate the text easily, displaying it in various ways that often reveal aspects of symbol usage not otherwise apparent. For example, one can display all sentences or other units of texts containing a particular word or phrase. Another use of computers is to count symbols, such as all occurrences of the phrase *United States.*

Although this monograph presents numerous examples of what was put into and produced by computers, it does not specify the instructions given (i.e., the computer programs). The Appendix, however, discusses several programs for text analysis and includes information on hardware compatibility and software sources. The Appendix also provides some information on publicly available text data bases that are in machine-readable form.

The first three chapters document a solid core of useful knowledge and tools for the analysis of text. There exist, however, several methodological problems that detract from the reliability of the text classification process or from the validity of the consequent interpretations and explanations. These problems — the subject of Chapter 4 — fall into four major categories: measurement, indication, representation, and interpretation.

Concluding Remarks

The spirit of the following material is illustrative and didactic rather than dogmatic. There is no simple *right way* to do content analysis. Instead, investigators must judge what methods are most appropriate for their substantive problems. Moreover, some technical problems in content analysis have yet to be resolved or are the subject of ongoing research and debate; a few of these problems are discussed in Chapter 4. Where possible, this monograph tries to state the problem clearly, to suggest alternative resolutions (if they are known), and to suggest what kinds of information or capacities might help resolve the matter.

Rather than presenting a summary of the existing literature, this monograph deliberately emphasizes material not covered or stressed elsewhere. The goal is to produce a more interesting and useful guide for those planning or actually doing research using content analysis. During the past 20 years, the introduction of inexpensive microcomputers, the introduction of cost-effective devices for making text machine-readable, and the general reduction of computer costs have renewed interest in content analysis. In the 1990s these tools will be applied increasingly to a wide range of social science questions.

As a brief introduction to content analysis, much has been omitted here. Consequently, there are suggestions for further reading at the end of each chapter. These sources address content analysis methods, substantive research, general issues in research methodology, or statistics at a much greater level of detail than is possible or even desirable here.

Suggestions for Further Reading

There are several books on content analysis that should be read by anyone seriously interested in the subject. Krippendorff (1980) surveys the field and its problems. It is especially useful for those doing human-coded content analysis. His discussion of reliability is "must" reading; the book is not up-to-date, however, regarding the use of computers.

Other books contain numerous methodological insights and practical information. One is the original book on the General Inquirer system (Stone, Dunphy, Smith, and Ogilvie, 1966), the first widely used computer system for content analysis. Although the version discussed there is not the current one (see Kelly and Stone, 1975; Zuell, Weber, and Mohler, 1989), the book presents a wide-ranging discussion of content analysis, its problems, and practical solutions. Stone and his associates also present several chapters illustrating the application of computer-aided content analysis to a variety of substantive problems. Namenwirth and Weber (1987) combine an in-depth consideration of content analysis methods with empirical analyses of political documents and speeches. The results are then interpreted and explained using several major social science theories. Another useful resource is a set of conference papers edited by Gerbner, Holsti, Krippendorff, Paisley, and Stone (1969). This interdisciplinary collection addresses many issues still current in content analysis. Also, Holsti's (1969) brief discussion remains worthwhile reading. North, Holsti, Zaninovich, and Zinnes (1963) apply a variety of content-analytic techniques to the study of communications in international relations. There exists an earlier, precomputer body of work on using content analysis, notably Berelson (1952); Lasswell, Leites, et al. (1965); Lasswell, Lerner, and Pool (1952); and Pool (1952a, 1952b, 1959). Smith (1978) employs coding rules and categories related to the Semantic Differential (Osgood, May, and Miron, 1975; Osgood, Suci, and Tannenbaum, 1957).

More popular accounts that use content analysis to assess cultural and social trends include Merriam and Makower (1988) and Naisbitt (1982). Gottschalk (1979) and Gottschalk, Lolas, and Vinex (1986) show the use of content analysis in behavioral and psychological research. Herzog (1973) shows that, over the past few decades, American political discourse has communicated less and less information (see Orwell, 1949). Williams (1985) gives an historical, social, and political account of certain *keywords* that figure prominently in contemporary social and political speech. His account might be useful in the construction of category schemes.

2. CONTENT CLASSIFICATION AND INTERPRETATION

The central problems of content analysis originate mainly in the data-reduction process by which the many words of texts are classified into much fewer content categories. One set of problems concerns the consistency or reliability of text classification. In content analysis, reliability problems usually grow out of the ambiguity of word meanings, category definitions, or other coding rules. Classification by multiple human coders permits the quantitative assessment of achieved reliability. Classification by computer, however, leads to perfect coder reliability (if one assumes valid computer programs and well-functioning computer hardware). Once correctly defined for the computer, the coding rules are always applied in the same way.

A much more difficult set of problems concerns the validity of variables based on content classification. A content analysis variable is valid to the extent that it measures the construct the investigator intends it to measure. As happens with reliability, validity problems also grow out of the ambiguity of word meanings and category or variable definitions.

As an introduction to these problems, consider two sample texts and some simple coding rules. Using commonsense definitions, imagine that the coding instructions define five categories: CITIZENS' RIGHTS, ECONOMIC, GOVERNMENT, POLITICAL DOCTRINE, and WELFARE. Imagine also that coders are instructed to classify each entire paragraph in one category only. Consider first a portion of the Carter 1980 Democratic Platform:

> Our current economic situation is unique. In 1977, we inherited a severe recession from the Republicans. The Democratic Administration and the Democratic Congress acted quickly to reduce the unacceptably high levels of unemployment and to stimulate the economy. And we succeeded. We recovered from that deep recession and our economy was strengthened and revitalized. As that fight was won, the enormous increases in foreign oil prices — 120 percent last year — and declining productivity fueled an

inflationary spiral that also had to be fought. The Democrats did that, and inflation has begun to recede. In working to combat these dual problems, significant economic actions have been taken. (Johnson, 1982: 38)

Now consider another paragraph from the Reagan 1980 Republican platform:

Through long association with government programs, the word "welfare" has come to be perceived almost exclusively as tax-supported aid to the needy. But in its most inclusive sense — and as Americans understood it from the beginning of the Republic — such aid also encompasses those charitable works performed by private citizens, families, and social, ethnic, and religious organizations. Policies of the federal government leading to high taxes, rising inflation, and bureaucratic empire-building have made it difficult and often impossible for such individuals and groups to exercise their charitable instincts. We believe that government policies that fight inflation, reduce tax rates, and end bureaucratic excesses can help make private effort by the American people once again a major force in those works of charity which are the true signs of a progressive and humane society. (Johnson, 1982: 179)

Most people would code the first excerpt in the ECONOMIC category, but the proper coding of the second is less obvious. This paragraph could be taken to be mainly about the rights of citizens, the desirability of restricting the government's role, the welfare state, or to be the espousal of a political doctrine. In fact, it occurs at the end of a section titled *Improving the Welfare System.*

The difficulty of classifying the second excerpt is contrived partly by the present author, because it results from the lack of clear and detailed coding rules for each category and from the variety of the subject matter. Large portions of text, such as paragraphs and complete texts, usually are more difficult to code as a unit than smaller portions, such as words and phrases, because large units typically contain more information and a greater diversity of topics. Hence they are more likely to present coders with conflicting cues.

These examples show the kind of difficulties investigators face with coding text. The next two sections look more systematically at coding problems, first from the perspective of reliability assessment and then from the perspective of validity assessment.

Reliability

Three types of reliability are pertinent to content analysis: stability, reproducibility, and accuracy (Krippendorff, 1980: 130-154). *Stability* refers to the extent to which the results of content classification are invariant over time. Stability can be determined when the same content is coded more than once by the *same* coder. Inconsistencies in coding constitute unreliability. These inconsistencies may stem from a variety of factors, including ambiguities in the coding rules, ambiguities in the text, cognitive changes within the coder, or simple errors, such as recording the wrong numeric code for a category. Because only one person is coding, stability is the weakest form of reliability.

Reproducibility, sometimes called *intercoder reliability,* refers to the extent to which content classification produces the same results when the same text is coded by *more than one* coder. Conflicting codings usually result from cognitive differences among the coders, ambiguous coding instructions, or from random recording errors. High reproducibility is a minimum standard for content analysis. This is because stability measures the consistency of the individual coder's private understandings, whereas reproducibility measures the consistency of shared understandings (or meaning) held by two or more coders.

Accuracy refers to the extent to which the classification of text corresponds to a standard or norm. It is the strongest form of reliability. As Krippendorff notes (1980: 131), it has sometimes been used to test the performance of human coders where a standard coding for some text has already been established. Except for training purposes, standard codings are established infrequently for texts. Consequently, researchers seldom use accuracy in reliability assessment.

Krippendorff (1980: 132) also points out that many investigators fail totally to assess the reliability of their coding. Even when reliability is assessed, some investigators engage in practices that often make data seem more reliable than they actually are. In particular, where coders have disagreed, investigators have resolved these disagreements by negotiations or by invoking the authority of the principal investigator or senior graduate assistant. Resolving these disagreements may produce judgments biased toward the opinions of the most verbal or more senior of the coders. Consequently, the reliability of the coding should be calculated *before* these disagreements are resolved. Krippendorff goes on to show several ways of calculating reliability for human coders. Readers who plan to do human-coded content analysis should pay close attention to Krippendorff's discussion. Later sections of this chapter return to reliability issues in conjunction with category construction and word classification.

Validity

The term *validity* is potentially confusing because it has been used in a variety of ways in the methods literature (see Brinberg and Kidder, 1982; Brinberg and McGrath, 1985; Campbell and Stanley, 1963; Cook and Campbell, 1979). Two distinctions, however, may help clarify the concept. The first is between validity as correspondence between two sets of things — such as concepts, variables, methods, and data — and validity as generalizability of results, references, and theory (Brinberg and McGrath, 1982). Correspondence and generalizability are themes that run throughout the following discussion of validity.

A second distinction, more specific to content analysis, is between the validity of the classification scheme, or variables derived from it, and the validity of the interpretation relating content variables to their causes or consequences. To assert that a category or variable (ECONOMIC, for example) is valid is to assert that there is a correspondence between the category and the abstract concept that it represents (concern with economic matters). To assert that a research result based on content analysis is valid is to assert that the finding does not depend upon or is generalizable beyond the specific data, methods, or measurements of a particular study. For instance, if a computer-assisted content analysis of party platforms shows a strong relationship between long-term economic fluctuations and concern with the well-being of economy and society, then the validity of the results would be greater to the extent that other data (e.g., newspaper editorials), other coding procedures (e.g., human rather than computer-coded), or other classification schemes (dictionaries) produced substantive conclusions.

Perhaps the weakest form of validity is *face* validity, which consists of the correspondence between investigators' definitions of concepts and their definitions of the categories that measured them. A category has face validity to the extent that it appears to measure the construct it is intended to measure. Even if several expert judges agree, face validity is still a weak claim because it rests on a single variable. Stronger forms of validity involve more than one variable. Unfortunately, content analysts often have relied heavily on face validity; consequently, some other social scientists have viewed their results skeptically.

Much stronger validity is obtained by comparing content-analytic data with some external criterion. Four types of external validity are pertinent.

A measure has *construct validity*[7] to the extent that it is correlated with some other measure of the same construct. Thus construct validity entails the generalizability of the construct across measures or methods. Campbell and Fiske (1959) and others (e.g., Althauser, 1974; Alwin, 1974; Campbell and O'Connell, 1982; Fiske, 1982) further differentiate *convergent* from *discriminant* validity. A measure has high construct validity when it correlates with other measures of the same construct (convergent) and is uncorrelated with measures of dissimilar constructs (discriminant).

The research reported in Saris-Gallhofer, Saris, and Morton (1978) is a fine example of applying these ideas to content-analytic data. The object of this study was to validate a content-analysis dictionary developed by Holsti (1969) using the main categories of the Semantic Differential (Anderson, 1970; Osgood, May, and Miron, 1975; Osgood, Suci, and Tannenbaum, 1957; Snider and Osgood, 1969). The semantic differential is a technique for assessing the primary categories people use in affective evaluation or classification. The details of the technique are not pertinent here. Investigations in this tradition, however, show that in a variety of cultures people use three basic dimensions of classification. Each of these dimensions is anchored by polar opposites:

- *evaluation* (positive versus negative affect)
- *potency* (strength versus weakness)
- *activity* (active versus passive)

Each word in Holsti's dictionary was assigned three numbers, each indicating its classification on one of the three dimensions of the semantic differential. Saris-Gallhofer and her colleagues compared Holsti's assignment of scores with Osgood's and with scores assigned by a group of students. Thus each word (or other unit of text) was classified by three different methods, with each method claiming to classify text on the same constructs. Using statistical techniques designed to assess convergent and discriminant validity, Saris-Gallhofer found that Holsti's scoring for the evaluation and potency dimensions was much more valid than his scoring for the activity dimension. It remains unclear why Holsti's scoring of the activity dimension is less valid than the scores for the other two. Additional research is required to determine the specific factors that affect the validity of content classification. Nonetheless, this study shows that sophisticated statistical techniques useful in accessing validity can be applied to content analysis data.

Hypothesis validity, the second type, relies on the correspondence among variables and the correspondence between these relationships and theory. A measure has hypothesis validity if in relationship to other variables it "behaves" as it is expected to.[8] For example, several studies based on political documents — such as party platform in presidential campaigns — have shown that the preoccupation of society with economic issues increases during bad economic times and decreases when the economy is good (e.g., Namenwirth, 1969b; Namenwirth and Weber, 1987). These results are consistent with theoretical arguments relating the cultural and social processes that generate political documents (such as party platforms) with changes in the economy. Thus the observed inverse relationship between economic fluctuations and concern with economic matters suggests the hypothesis validity of measured variables and of the constructs that they represent.

A measure has *predictive validity,* the third type, to the extent that forecasts about events or conditions external to the study are shown to correspond to actual events or conditions. These predictions may concern future, past (postdiction), or concurrent events. Predictive validity is powerful because the inferences from data are generalized successfully beyond the study to situations not under the direct control of the investigator.

Content-analytic data are seldom shown to have predictive validity,[9] but three examples illustrate the point:

1. Ogilvie, Stone, and Shneidman (1966) analyzed real suicide notes from 33 males who had been matched for age, gender, occupation, religion, and ethnicity with 33 nonsuicidal controls who were asked to produce simulated suicide notes. Using General Inquirer-type computer-aided content analysis, Stone was able to correctly distinguish real from simulated suicide notes in 30 of the 33 pairs (90.9%) of notes.

2. George (1959a) studied inferences made by The Foreign Broadcast Intelligence Service of the FCC from German Propaganda during the Second World War. He found that Allied intelligence analysts often could

anticipate changes in German war tactics and strategy from changes in the content of radio broadcasts and other media.

3. Namenwirth's (1973) analysis of party platforms in presidential campaigns, written in the late 1960s, suggested that America would experience severe economic difficulties that would peak about 1980. Events since seem to confirm this prediction.

Words or other coding units classified together need to possess similar connotations in order for the classification to have *semantic validity,* the fourth and final type. According to Krippendorff (1980: 159ff), semantic validity exists when persons familiar with the language and texts examine lists of words (or other units) placed in the same category and agree that these words have similar meanings or connotations.

Although this seems an obvious requirement for valid content analysis, many difficulties arise because words and category definitions are sometimes ambiguous. For example, some systems for computer-aided content analysis cannot distinguish among the various senses of words with more than one meaning, such as *mine.* Does this refer to a hole in the ground, the process of extraction, or a possessive pronoun? Because of this failure, word counts including the frequency of *mine* lack semantic validity. Various aspects of semantic validity are discussed later in this and in subsequent chapters.

Creating and Testing
a Coding Scheme

Many studies require investigators to design and implement coding schemes. Whether the coding is to be done by humans or by computer, the process of creating and applying a coding scheme consists of several basic steps. If investigators have identified the substantive questions to be investigated, relevant theories, previous research, and the texts to be classified, they next proceed with the following necessary steps:

1. *Define the recording units.* One of the most fundamental and important decisions concerns the definition of the basic unit of text to be classified. There are six commonly used options:

- *Word*—One choice is to code each word. As noted, some computer software for text analysis cannot distinguish among the various senses of words with more than one meaning, and hence may produce erroneous conclusions.

- *Word sense* — Other computer programs are able to code the different senses of words with multiple meanings and to code phrases that constitute a semantic unit, such as idioms (e.g., *taken for granted*) or proper nouns (e.g., *the Empire State Building*). These issues are discussed in detail later.

- *Sentence* — An entire sentence is often the recording unit when the investigator is interested in words or phrases that occur closely together. For example, coders may be instructed to count sentences in which either positive, negative, or affectively neutral references are made to the Soviet Union. A sentence with the phrase *evil empire* would be counted as NEGATIVE EVALUATION, whereas *Talks with the Soviet Union continue* would be coded NEUTRAL EVALUATION, and *The President supports recent efforts to extend economic and political rights in the Soviet Union* would be coded POSITIVE EVALUATION.

- *Theme* — Holsti (1963: 136, emphasis in the original) defines a theme as a unit of text "having *no more than one each of the following elements:* (1) the *perceiver,* (2) the *perceived* or agent of action, (3) the *action,* (4) the *target* of the action." For example, the sentence *The President / hates / Communists* would be divided as shown. Numeric or other codes often are inserted in the text to represent subject / verb / object. This form of coding preserves important information and provides a means of distinguishing between the sentence above and the assertion that *Communists hate the President.*

Sometimes long, complex sentences must be broken down into shorter thematic units or segments. Here, parts of speech shared between themes must be repeated. Also, ambiguous phrases and pronouns must be identified manually. These steps are taken before coding for the content. Holsti (1963: 136-137) gives the following example of editing more complex sentences before coding for themes and content:[10]

The sentence, "The American imperialists have perverted the peace and are preparing to attack the Socialist Camp," must be edited to read: The American imperialists have perverted the peace + (the Americans) are preparing to attack the Socialist Camp."

This form of coding is labor-intensive, but leads to much more detailed and sophisticated comparisons. See Holsti (1963, 1966, 1969) for further details.

- *Paragraph* — When computer assistance is not feasible and when resources for human coding are limited, investigators sometimes code entire paragraphs to reduce the effort required. Evidence discussed later in this chapter shows that it is more difficult to achieve high reliability when coding large units, such as paragraphs, than when coding smaller units, such as words.

- *Whole text* — Unless the entire text is short — like newspaper headlines, editorials, or stories — it is difficult to achieve high reliability when coding complete texts.

2. *Define the categories.* In creating category definitions, investigators must make two basic decisions. (Other related issues are taken up later.) The first is whether the categories are to be mutually exclusive. Most statistical procedures require variables that are not confounded. If a recording unit can be classified simultaneously in two or more categories and if both categories (variables) are included in the same statistical analysis, then it is possible that, because the basic statistical assumptions of the analysis are violated, the results are dubious. This is likely to be the case when using common multivariate procedures such as factor analysis, analysis of variance, and multiple regression.

The second choice concerns how narrow or broad the categories are to be. Some categories are limited because of language. For example, a category indicating self-references defined as first person singular pronouns will have only a few words or entries. A category defined as concern with ECONOMIC matters may have many entries. For some purposes, however, it may make sense to use much more narrow or specific categories, such as INFLATION, TAXES, BUDGET, TRADE, AGRICULTURE, and so on.

3. *Test coding on sample of text.* The best test of the clarity of category definitions is to code a small sample of the text. Testing not only reveals ambiguities in the rules, but also often leads to insights suggesting revisions of the classification scheme.

4. *Assess accuracy or reliability. Accuracy* in this sense means the text is coded correctly by the computer, not in the sense of the type of reliability that was discussed earlier. If human coders are used, the reliability of the coding process should be estimated *before* resolving disputes among the coders.

5. *Revise the coding rules.* If the reliability is low, or if errors in computer procedures are discovered, the coding rules must be revised or the software corrected.

6. *Return to Step 3.* This cycle will continue until the coders achieve sufficient reliability or until the computer procedures work correctly.

7. *Code all the text.* When high coder reliability has been achieved or when the computer programs are functioning correctly, the coding rules can then be applied to all the text.

8. *Assess achieved reliability or accuracy.* The reliability of human coders should be assessed after the text is classified. Never assume that if samples of text were coded reliably then the entire corpus of text will also be coded reliably. Human coders are subject to fatigue and are likely to make more mistakes as the coding proceeds. Also, as the text is coded, their understanding of the coding rules may change in subtle ways that lead to greater unreliability.

If the coding was done by computer, the output should be checked carefully to insure that the coding rules were applied correctly. Text not in the sample(s) used for testing may present novel combinations of words that were not anticipated or encountered earlier, and these may be misclassified.

Dictionaries and Computerized
Text Classification

Content analysts have used several strategies to create categories and variables. Some investigators have counted by hand a few key words or phrases. Tufte (1978: 75), for example, counted certain words in the 1976 Democratic and Republican party platforms, including indicators of distributional issues (such as *inequity, regressive, equal,* and *redistribution*) and indicators of concern with inflation (such as *inflation, inflationary, price stability,* and *rising prices*).

Others have constructed a set of content categories on the basis of a single concept. For example, the early version of Stone's General Inquirer computer system was used to analyze achievement imagery (McClelland's N-Achievement; Stone, Dunphy, Smith, and Ogilvie, 1966: 191ff). This approach offers several advantages. It permits the intensive and detailed analysis of a single theoretical construct. It also provides an explicit rationale not only for what is retained, but also for what is excluded from the analysis. Furthermore, single-concept coding schemes often have high validity and reliability.

Another approach to content analysis involves the creation and application of general dictionaries.[11] Content-analysis dictionaries consist of category names, the definitions or rules for assigning words to categories, and the actual assignment of specific words. This strategy provides the researcher with numerous categories (60 to 150+) into which most words in most texts can be classified.[12] Once created, general dictionaries are advantageous because they:

- provide a wide range of categories to choose from (see Stone et al., 1966: 42-44)
- minimize the time needed for dictionary construction, validation, and revision
- standardize classification
- encourage the accumulation of comparable results when used in many studies[13]

It is worth noting that dictionary construction commonly is misperceived to be merely a preface or preparatory step for quantification. While researchers frequently use dictionaries to define variables for quantification, they also use categories to locate and retrieve text by finding occurrences of semantically equivalent symbols. Chapter 3 presents examples of retrievals based on categories.

Certain problems arise in the creation of *any* content category or set of categories. These problems stem from the ambiguity of both the category definitions and the words that are to be assigned to categories. To aid discussion of these difficulties, two general dictionaries are used as examples: the Harvard IV Psychosocial Dictionaries, developed by Dexter Dunphy and his associates (Dunphy, Bullard, and Crossing, 1989; Kelly and Stone, 1975; Zuell, Weber, and Mohler, 1989), and the Lasswell Value Dictionary (LVD), developed and extended by J. Zvi Namenwirth and his associates (Namenwirth and Weber, 1987; Zuell et al., 1989). Both dictionaries are used with Stone's General Inquirer system for the analysis of English language text.[14]

Tables 2.1 and 2.2 present definitions of selected content categories from the LVD and Harvard IV-4 dictionaries, respectively.[15] Categories often are represented by abbreviations or tags, which appear in these tables. The process of classifying words in texts is often called *tagging*. The categories that appear in these tables show similarities and differences between the dictionaries and introduce the analysis of sample text presented below and in Chapter 3.

For instance, one set of LVD categories contains those words, word senses,[16] and idioms that denote wealth-related matters. Another category contains wealth words indicating a transaction or exchange of

TABLE 2.1

Selected Lasswell Value Dictionary Categories

Tag	Full Name and Definition
ENLSCOP	ENLIGHTENMENT-SCOPE-INDICATOR: Words indicating concern with wisdom, knowledge, etc. as a fundamental goal rather than a means to other ends.
ENLTOT	ENLIGHTENMENT-TOTAL: Indicates concern with knowledge, insight and information concerning cultural and personal relations. Includes all entries denoting and describing academic matters and the processes that generate and communicate information, thought, and understanding.
NTYPE	N-TYPE WORDS: Relatively high frequency words that often lack semantic meaning, e.g., *a, the, to*, forms of the verb *to be*.
SCOPIND	SCOPE-INDICATOR: Indicates concern with ultimate ends rather than with means.
SELVES	SELVES: First person plural pronouns.
SKLTOT	SKILL-TOTAL: SKILL is defined as proficiency in any practice whatever, whether in arts or crafts, trade or profession. Indicates a concern with the mastery of the physical environment and the skills and tools used to that purpose.
SURE	SURE: Sentiment category containing words that indicate certainty, sureness, and firmness.
TIMESP	TIME-SPACE: General time and space category. Contains directions, e.g., *up, down*, etc., and time indicators, e.g., *hour, early, late*.
UNDEF	UNDEFINED: Includes words with value implications that vary from context to context, and which, notwithstanding disambiguation routes, cannot be assessed reliably by present procedures.
UNDEF*	UNDEFINABLE: Includes entries which have no value implications or which have value meaning which cannot be defined in terms of the present category scheme.
WLTOTH	WEALTH-OTHER: Entries denoting the wealth process not classified as PARTICIPANT or TRANSACTION are classified here.
WLTPT	WEALTH-PARTICIPANT: Contains the generic names of the trades and professions in the wealth process. Also includes social roles related to wealth processes, e.g., *banker*.
WLTTOT	WEALTH-TOTAL: Wealth is defined as income or services of goods and persons accruing to the person in any way whatsoever. All references to production resources and the accumulation or exchange of goods and services have been included in this category.
WLTXACT	WEALTH-TRANSACTION: Contains references to the creation or exchange of wealth, mainly verbs.
XACT	TRANSACTION: Residual category indicating value transactions not classified elsewhere because it could not be determined reliably whether the transaction resulted in a gain or loss or what was the object of the transaction.

TABLE 2.2

Selected Harvard IV Dictionary Categories

Tag	Full Name and Definition
AFFIL	AFFILIATION: All words with the connotation of affiliation or supportiveness.
BEGIN	BEGIN: Words indicating beginning.
CAUSAL	CAUSAL: Words denoting presumption that occurrence of one phenomenon necessarily is preceded, accompanied, or followed by the occurrence of another.
COLL	COLLECTIVITY: All-collectivities excluding animal collectivities (ANIMAL).
COMFORM	COMMUNICATION FORM: All processes and forms of communication, excluding finite, concrete, visible, and tangible objects for communication, e.g., *book*, but does include words such as *essay, fare*, and *chapter*, where the emphasis is more on the communication transaction than on the object itself.
COMN	COMMUNICATION: All forms and processes of communication.
DOCTR	DOCTRINE: Organized systems of belief or knowledge. Includes all formal bodies of knowledge (*astronomy, agriculture*), belief systems (*Christianity, stoicism*), the arts.
ECON*	ECONOMIC: All words which relate to economic, commercial, and industrial matters. Includes all economic roles, collectivities, acts, abstract ideas, and symbols. Also includes references to technical industrial processes and to economic commodities such as coal and aluminum.
EXCH	EXCHANGE: Words indicating economic processes and transactions such as buying and selling.
GOAL	GOAL: Names of end-states toward which striving, muscular or mental, is directed.
IMPERS	IMPERSONAL: All impersonal nouns.
INCR	INCREASE: Words indicating increase.
INTREL	INTERRELATE: Interpersonal action words involving changing relationships between people, things, or ideas. Abstract nouns derived from these verbs are to be found generally in VIRTUE or VICE.
OUR	OUR: All pronouns which are inclusive self-references.
OVRST	OVERSTATE: Words providing emphasis in the following areas: speed, frequency, inevitability, causality, inclusiveness of persons, objects, or places, quantity in numerical and quasi-numerical terms, accuracy and validity, importance, intensity, likelihood, certainty, and extremity.
POLIT*	POLITICAL: All words with a clearly political character. Includes political roles, collectivities, acts, ideas, ideologies, and symbols.
POWER	POWER: All words with the connotation of power, control, or authority.

value (WEALTH-TRANSACTIONS), such as forms of the verbs *buy, sell,* and *mortgage.* A third category contains words that name a role or person involved in wealth matters (WEALTH-PARTICIPANTS), such as *banker, buyer,* and *seller.*

Reliability and Classification Schemes

As noted, the construction of valid and useful content categories depends on the interaction between language and the classification scheme (Namenwirth and Weber, 1987). For example, one often can think of categories for which only a few words exist, such as a category for first person singular pronouns (e.g., SELF in the LVD). To avoid difficulties in statistical estimation[17] resulting from categories with limited numbers of words, the LVD aggregates the remaining wealth-related words, word senses, and idioms indicating a concern with wealth into a WEALTH-OTHER category. Finally, all the WEALTH subcategories are combined into a category indicating the overall concern with economic matters, WEALTH-TOTAL. In comparison (Table 2.3), the Harvard IV-4 dictionary scheme provides only two similar categories, ECONOMIC and EXCHANGE. Another perspective on classification schemes is gained by examining the assignment of words to categories. Table 2.3 presents a portion of the alphabetic list of nouns assigned to WEALTH-OTHER. The LVD originally was constructed primarily for the analysis of political documents, such as newspaper editorials and party platforms. Thus the WEALTH-OTHER category includes many nouns that refer to commodities, such as *corn, tin,* and so forth because in political documents references to these commodities occur in an economic context (e.g., *The price of corn declined for the seventh consecutive month*).

The numbers at the end of some words indicate the particular sense number of a word with more than one meaning (i.e., a homograph). They are not immediately useful without a corresponding list of the various senses of each homograph, but space limitations preclude an extensive discussion here (the interested reader is referred to Kelly and Stone, 1975; Zuell et al., 1989).

Although categories about economic matters generally have high internal consistency in the sense that all the words have similar connotations, this is not necessarily the case with other categories. For example, the LVD lumps together words related to temporal and spatial relations. The justification for this has always been vague, and perhaps there should be a separate category for each. Similarly, the Harvard

TABLE 2.3

Alphabetical Listing of WEALTH-OTHER Nouns,
(Lasswell Value Dictionary)

NOUNS			
ABUNDANCE	DEPRESSION#2	IRRIGATION	RESOURCE
ACCOUNT#2	DOLLAR	LEDGER	RETAIL#1
ACRE	EARN#2	LIABILITY#1	RETIREMENT
AFFLUENCE	ECONOMICS	LIVESTOCK	RETURN#3
AGRICULTURE	ECONOMIST	LOAN#1	RICH#6
ALLOWANCE	ECONOMY	LOT#3	ROAD#1
ANNUITY	ELECTRICITY	LOW-COST	ROYALTY#2
APPROPRIATION	EMPLOYMENT	LUXURY	RUBBER
ARTICLE#2	END#6	MANUFACTURE#1	SALARY
AUTO	ENDOWMENT	MANUFACTURER	SALESMANSHIP
AUTOMOBILE	ENERGY	MARKET#1	SAVE#3
BACKWARDNESS	ENGINE	MARKET#2	SCARCITY
BALE	ENTERPRISE	MERCHANDISE	SECURITY#2
BANKRUPTCY	EQUITY	MINE#2	SECURITY#3
BARGAIN#1	ESTATE	MINERAL	SELL#2
BELONG#2	EXPENDITURE	MINT	SHIFT#2
BENEFIT#1	EXPENSE#1	MONEY	SHOP#1
BILL#2	EXPORT#1	MORTGAGE#1	SHOP#3
BONUS	FACTORY	OIL	SILK
BOOKKEEPING	FARM#1	ORE	STEEL
BOUNTY	FARM#3	OUTPUT#1	STERLING
BRANCH#2	FERTILIZER	OWNERSHIP	STOCK
BRASS	FINANCE#1	PARITY	STORE#1
BREAD	FOREST	PAY#2	STORE#3
BUDGET	FORESTRY	PAYROLL	SUPPLIER
BUSINESS#1	FORTUNE#2	PENNY	SUPPLY#1
BUY#2	FREIGHT	PENSION	SURPLUS
CAPITAL	FRUGALITY	PIECE#2	TARIFF
CAR	FUND#1	PLANT#2	TAX#1
CARTEL	FUND#2	PLANTATION	TAX#3
CASH#1	FUR	POOR#5	TAX#4
CATTLE	GARDEN#1	POPULATION	TAXATION
CENT	GARDEN#2	PORT	TEXTILE
CHARGE#4	GIFT	POULTRY	TIMBER
CHECK#1	GOLD	POUND#1	TIN
CHEQUE	GOODS	POVERTY	TRAIN#1
CLEAR#10	GRAIN	PRESENT#5	TRANSPORT#1
COAL	GRANT#1	PRICE	TRANSPORTATION
COFFEE	HERD#1	PROCEED#3	TREASURE#1
COIN	HIDE#3	PRODUCE#2	TREASURER
COLLATERAL	HIGHWAY	PRODUCER	TREASURY
COMMERCE	HOLD#4	PRODUCTIVITY	TRUST#5
COMMODITY	HORTICULTURE	PROPERTY	UNEMPLOYMENT
COPPER	HOUSEHOLD	PROSPERITY	WAGE#1
COPYRIGHT	INCENTIVE	RANCH	WEALTH#1
CORN	INCOME#1	RANCHER	WHEAT
COTTON	INDEMNITY	RATE#1	WHOLESALE
CROP#1	INDUSTRIALISM	REAL#3	WIN#3
CURRENCY	INDUSTRY	RECEIPT	WOOD#1
CUSTOM#2	INFLATION	RECLAMATION	WOOD#2
DEBT	INPUT	REDEVELOPMENT	WOOL
DEFICIT	INTEREST#2	REFUND#1	WORTH#3
DEPARTMENT#2	INVENTORY	REMUNERATION	
DEPRECIATION	INVESTMENT	RENT#1	
	IRON#1	RENTAL	

dictionary classifies words that refer to political ideologies and to political actors in the same category. Again, the justification for this strategy is unclear.

Whether to extend the effort required to resolve these kinds of difficulties will depend on the goals of specific investigations. For example, if *time* is an important concept, then separate categories for *space* and *time* will be desirable.

Even if the ambiguity of category definitions and word classifications can be overcome, other potential sources of error remain. As noted, one of the most serious problems in some computer programs for content analysis is that they cannot deal with words that have more than one meaning (i.e., homographs). For example, does *kind* refer to class of objects or a benevolent disposition? For English-language text, these problems are resolved by the latest version of the General Inquirer system (Kelly and Stone, 1975; Zuell et al., 1989). These computer programs and their associated dictionaries — the Harvard IV and the LVD — incorporate rules that distinguish among the various senses of homographs according to the context of usage. Technically known as *disambiguation rules,* these procedures lead to an important increase in the precision of text classification. In this context, higher precision refers to higher accuracy resulting from more or finer distinctions.[18]

Another problem in text analysis arises from phrases or idioms that constitute a single unit of meaning. Some of these are proper noun phrases — for example, *Sage Publications, United Nations,* or *United States of America.* Others are idioms or phrases such as *bleeding-heart liberals, point of no return,* or *a turn for the worst.* Whereas the earliest forms of the General Inquirer included the capability to handle idioms, the latest version uses the same flexible features for handling homographs to handle idioms. Thus the investigator can choose from among the individual word, word sense (of homographs), or phrase as the appropriate semantic unit.[19]

Although some computer systems handle the ambiguity of homographs, there exist other unresolved difficulties with this type of text classification. Because this software operates on only one sentence at a time, it cannot determine the referents of pronouns and ambiguous phrases (such as *we* or *dual problems* in the last sentence of the first example at the beginning of this chapter). Two resolutions of this problem have been commonly employed. The first is to ignore it, with the consequence that some category counts are slight underestimations. The second strategy is to edit the text so that the referent is placed immediately after the pronoun or phrases. This method is labor-intensive, but leads to more accurate counts.[20] Here is an excerpt from the 1886 address of the British monarch before Parliament (similar to our State of the Union address) discussing Home Rule for Ireland with the referent of *it* identified by the investigator (adapted from Namenwirth and Weber, 1987: 108):

> I have seen with deep sorrow the renewal, since I last addressed you, of the attempt to excite the people of Ireland to hostility against the legislative union between that country and Great Britain. I am resolutely opposed to any disturbance of the fundamental law, and in resisting it [any disturbance of the fundamental law] I am convinced that I shall be heartily supported by my Parliament and my people.

TABLE 2.4

Sample Text with LVD Tags

Word	Categories
SENTENCE 7 ** DOCUMENT 1 ** IDENTIFICATION AD1980	
THE	N-TYPE
EFFECT#1	SCOPE-INDICATOR
ON	N-TYPE
OUR	SELVES
ECONOMY	WEALTH-OTHER WEALTH-TOTAL
MUST#1	UNDEFINED
BE#1	N-TYPE
ONE#2	UNDEFINABLE
WHICH	N-TYPE
ENCOURAGE#1S	POWER-INDULGENCE POWER-TOTAL
JOB	SKILL-OTHER SKILL-TOTAL
FORMATION	UNDEFINED
AND	N-TYPE
BUSINESS#1	WEALTH-OTHER WEALTH-TOTAL
GROWTH.	SCOPE-INDICATOR
*** START NEW DOCUMENT..	
SENTENCE 8 ** DOCUMENT 2 ** IDENTIFICATION AR1980	
TAX#1ES.	WEALTH-OTHER WEALTH-TOTAL
SENTENCE 9 ** DOCUMENT 2 ** IDENTIFICATION AR1980	
ELSEWHERE	TIME-SPACE
IN	N-TYPE
THIS#1	N-TYPE
PLATFORM#1	POWER-OTHER POWER-TOTAL
WE	SELVES
DISCUSS	ENLIGHTENMENT-SCOPE-INDICATOR ENLIGHTENMENT-TOTAL
THE	N-TYPE
BENEFIT#3S	BASE-INDICATOR
FOR	N-TYPE
SOCIETY	COLLECTIVE-PARTICIPANT
AS#1	N-TYPE
A	N-TYPE
WHOLE#2,	UNDEFINED
OF	N-TYPE
REDUCED	TRANSACTION
TAXATION,	WEALTH-OTHER WEALTH-TOTAL
PARTICULAR#4LY	SURE
IN	N-TYPE
TERM#1S	ENLIGHTENMENT-OTHER ENLIGHTENMENT-TOTAL
OF	N-TYPE
ECONOMIC	WEALTH-OTHER WEALTH-TOTAL
GROWTH.	SCOPE-INDICATOR

Table 2.4 presents a few sentences from the 1980 party platforms. Each word is followed by a list of assigned LVD categories.[21] As in the previous table, the numbers next to some words indicate the particular sense of homographs. A significant portion of the text consists of words that are important for the construction of sentences, but are not assigned to substantive LVD categories. These N-TYPE words include articles (e.g. *a, the*) and some prepositions (e.g., *in, of*). Indices usually are constructed after subtracting the number of N-TYPE words from the total number of words. For example, dividing the number of words in a document classified in a particular category by the total minus N-TYPE number of words in the document yields a measure interpreted as the proportion of words with relevant semantic information classified in that category.

Additional problems arise because some words may be classified in two categories, where one is a total and the other is a subcategory. *Economy,* for example, is classified as WEALTH-OTHER and WEALTH-TOTAL. As noted, to maintain the mathematical independence of the content variables, investigators should analyze either the total category or one or more subcategories, but not both the total and one or more subcategories in the same statistical procedure.

A major advantage of computer-aided content analysis is that the same text can be analyzed easily using more than one category scheme. Also, because of errors or because changes seem justified in light of the particular text being analyzed, the text can be reclassified after making modifications to an existing dictionary. Table 2.5 presents the text from Table 2.4 classified according to the categories of the Harvard IV-4 dictionary. Again, the output consists of words with the sense numbers of homographs and a list of assigned Harvard IV categories.[22]

Several ways of manipulating, classifying, and analyzing text are presented in Chapter 3. The remainder of this chapter discusses several important problems in the construction of category schemes and text classification.

Single Versus Multiple Classification

In classifying a word or other recording unit into a particular dictionary category, one really answers the question: Does the entry generally have a certain attribute (or set of interrelated attributes)? Two answers to this question exist: yes, the entry does, and therefore it is classified thus; or no, and therefore the entry is not classified under this heading.

TABLE 2.5

Sample Text with Harvard IV Tags

Word	Categories
SENTENCE 7 ** DOCUMENT 1 ** IDENTIFICATION AD1980	
THE	ARTICLE
EFFECT#1	ABSTRACT CAUSAL PSV
ON	SPACE
OUR	AFFILIATION OUR
ECONOMY	DOCTRINE ECONOMIC
MUST#1	OUGHT
BE#1	BE
ONE#2	INDEF OTHER
WHICH	INDEF INT RLTVI
ENCOURAGE#1S	INTERRELATEL AFFILIATION PSTV ACTV
JOB	MEANS ECONOMIC
FORMATION	MEANS STRNG
AND	CONJ1
BUSINESS#1	DOCTRINE ECONOMIC
GROWTH.	STRNG INCR PSV
*** START NEW DOCUMENT..	
SENTENCE 8 ** DOCUMENT 2 ** IDENTIFICATION AR1980	
TAX#1ES.	MEANS POLIT ECONOMIC
SENTENCE 9 ** DOCUMENT 2 ** IDENTIFICATION AR1980	
ELSEWHERE	SPACE
IN	SPACE
THIS#1	DEM DEM1
PLATFORM#1	DOCTRINE POLITICAL
WE	PLRLP OUR
DISCUSS	PSTV COMFORM
THE	ARTICLE
BENEFIT#3S,	GOAL PSTV STRNG
FOR	CONJ CONJ2
SOCIETY	COLL POLITICAL
AS#1	CONJ2 CAUSAL
A	ARTICLE
WHOLE#2,	QUAN STRNG OVRST
OF	PREP
REDUCED	DECR STRNG
TAXATION,	MEANS POLIT ECONOMIC
PARTICULAR#4LY	OVRST
IN	SPACE
TERM#1S	COM COMFORM
OF	PREP
ECONOMIC	POLIT DOCTRINE ECONOMIC
GROWTH.	STRNG INCR PSV

This formulation points at two complications. First, having one attribute logically does not exclude the possession of another. Second, not all entries need have the same attribute to the same extent; the qualities by which words are classified may be continuous rather than dichotomous, thus leading to variation in intensity.[23] Double or multiple classification of entries resolves the first problem, but creates others.

Different strategies have been followed to resolve these issues. For example, the design of the Lasswell dictionary assumes that the gain in semantic precision does not outweigh the loss of logical distinctiveness and exclusiveness (Namenwirth and Weber, 1987; Zuell et al., 1989). Logical exclusiveness is a precarious precondition of all classification for subsequent statistical analysis. Therefore, in the Lasswell dictionary, if an entry can be classified under more than one category it is classified in the category that seems most appropriate — most of the time — for most texts. As for intensity, although it is true that not all entries will reflect the category to the same extent, Namenwirth and Weber (1987) chose a dichotomous rather than a weighted classification scheme because no reliable method for assigning weights or intensity scores could be perfected.

The category scheme of the current Harvard dictionaries was constructed using a very different strategy (Dunphy et al., 1989). They have a set of *first-order* categories to which entries can be assigned on a hierarchical basis if warranted. These first-order categories represent the basic analytic categories. Figure 2.1 illustrates the hierarchical nature of the Harvard IV-4 first-order categories that deal with psychological states. Two categories, NEED and PERCEIVE, have no subcategories, but FEEL, THINK, and EVALUATE do.

The Harvard dictionary contains another set of categories, called *second-order* categories that are independent of the first, and provide alternative modes of classification. For example, there is a set of second-order categories derived from the Osgood semantic differential discussed earlier. How, then, are words classified using this architecture? The word *abstract* is classified in both THINK and its subcategory KNOW. *Absence* is categorized in the same two categories with the addition of WEAK, one of the Osgood categories. *Acceptable* is classified in the first-order THINK and EVALUATE, the EVALUATE subcategory VIRTUE, and the Osgood POSITIVE category.

Although this type of scheme provides a multitude of possibilities for the investigator, great care must be taken if multivariate statistical

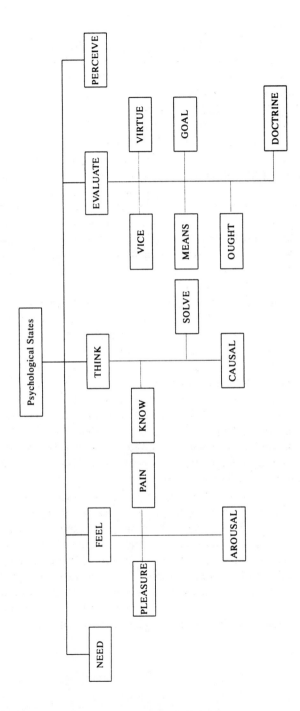

Figure 2.1. Harvard IV Dictionary First-Order Categories: Psychological States.

procedures will be used to analyze category counts, because the categories and the variables based on them may not be mutually exclusive.

Even if the category definition is precise, the decision to classify a particular word in a category often is difficult because of ambiguities in word meaning. Word ambiguity poses two problems. As noted above, a word may have multiple meanings. Also, a word may not seem as strong an indicator of a category as other similar words. Consider the LVD category SURE (similar to the Harvard category OVERSTATE), which contains words indicating certainty, sureness, and firmness. Words such as *certainly, sure,* and *emphatically* fit the definition quite well. But what about *authoritative* and *doctrinaire,* which in one thesaurus are also listed under "certainty"? In the LVD, *authoritative* is categorized with words indicating a concern with authoritative power (POWER-AUTHORITATIVE), whereas *doctrinaire* is categorized with words indicating a concern with doctrines and ideologies (POWER-DOCTRINE).

In some instances the investigator may decide that certain words clearly represent a particular category, that other words indicate or represent a category less strongly than words in the first group, while still other words seem to belong in more than one category. Many proposals exist to resolve these problems (Namenwirth and Weber, 1987: chapter 8), but none are entirely satisfactory. One solution is to weight each word depending on how well it connotes the category. Advocates of this strategy, however, never have provided a convincing argument demonstrating how valid weights can be determined reliably. An alternate solution is to categorize some words in more than one category. This strategy may lead to conceptually fuzzy categories, which, as noted, lack statistical independence.

Perhaps the best practical strategy is to classify each word, word sense, or phrase in the category where it most clearly belongs. If there is sufficient ambiguity, the word should be dropped from the category and — if necessary — from analysis. This tactic restricts categories to those words that unmistakably indicate concern with the category, thereby maximizing validity. Some words of substantive interest, however, may not be analyzed because they are not clear indicators of a particular category. Each investigator will have to find the resolution that makes the most sense in light of the goals of the analysis.

Assumed Versus Inferred Categories

Compared with hand coding, computer-based content analysis has the advantage that one set of texts can be classified easily by more than one dictionary. This, however, generates multiple descriptions of the same textual reality. Consequently, an important debate exists over whose classification scheme should be used. Some (Dunphy et al., 1989; Stone et al., 1966) hold that the category scheme should be justified theoretically; therefore, the investigator's categories should be used. For example, the earliest Harvard Psychosocial dictionaries were based in part on Parsonian and Freudian concepts (Stone et al., 1966) whereas the Lasswell Value Dictionary (Namenwirth and Weber, 1987; Zuell et al., 1989) is predicated on Lasswell and Kaplan's (1950) conceptual scheme for political analysis.[24]

Others (e.g., Cleveland, McTavish, and Pirro, 1974; Iker and Harway, 1969; Krippendorff, 1980: 126) argue that assumed category schemes impose the reality of the investigator on the text and that the better course of action uses the categories of those who produced the text.[25] These categories frequently are inferred from covariation among high-frequency words using factor analysis or similar techniques.[26]

This dispute stems both from difficult methodological problems and from conceptual confusion. Specifically, let the term *category* be reserved for groups of words with *similar* meanings and/or connotations (Dunphy et al., 1989; Stone et al., 1966). The words *banker, money,* and *mortgage* might be classified in a WEALTH or ECONOMIC category. Now let the term *theme* refer to clusters of words with *different* meanings or connotations that taken together refer to some theme or issue. For instance, the sentence *New York bankers invest money in many industries both at home and abroad* in part reflects concern with an economic theme. This disagreement over categories is largely a dispute between those who define categories as words with different meanings or connotations that covary empirically (inferred categories) and those who define categories as words with similar meanings or connotations that do not covary (assumed categories). Words classified as ECONOMIC, for example, will tend to covary with words in other categories, say POWER, UNCERTAINTY, or WELL-BEING, rather than with other ECONOMIC words.

Terminology aside, in studies using inferred categories, different category schemes arise from different sets of texts. Advocates of interred categories have failed to recognize that this multitude of categories requires a theory of categories. Such a theory would explain the range of possible categories and the empirically observed variation in category schemes (Namenwirth and Weber, 1987). Without such a theory, research using inferred categories is unlikely to lead to the cumulation of comparable results.

Alternate Classification Schemes and Substantive Results

The choice of classification schemes is in part predicated on theoretical considerations. For example, if one wishes to study exclusively a particular construct, such as McClelland's Need Achievement (Nach), then one might construct a dictionary that scores only that variable (e.g., Stone et al., 1966: 191ff). General dictionaries follow a different strategy based on many commonsense categories of meaning. These categories are chosen to reflect the wide range of human experience and understanding encoded in language.

Having decided to use the strategy of general dictionaries, the choice of one rather than another content classification scheme has little or no effect on the substantive results. That is, if the same text is classified using different general dictionaries (and analogous measurement models; see Namenwirth and Weber, 1987: chapter 8), then one will arrive at the same substantive conclusions.

Empirical evidence supports this point (Namenwirth and Bibbee, 1975: 61). In their analysis of newspaper editorials, Namenwirth and Bibbee classified the text using two different dictionaries and then factor analyzed the two sets of scores separately. Comparing the results across dictionaries, they found that the factors had similar interpretations. Furthermore, irrespective of which dictionary was used, Namenwirth and Bibbee arrived at similar substantive conclusions.[27]

This evidence is suggestive rather than conclusive. Consequently, future research should investigate the relationship between the dictionary used to classify text and the substantive conclusions. Texts can be classified with more than one dictionary and the results compared. If the results only partially replicate across dictionaries, additional research should determine the circumstances under which the results are similar and variant. Also, if the substantive conclusions do not depend on the particular category scheme, researchers reluctant to use one or another existing dictionary that does not operationalize their particular conceptual scheme might now be persuaded to do so. In addition, those who might create dictionaries in languages other than English might be persuaded to use existing category schemes to maintain cross-language comparability of results.

Units of Aggregation Problems

After assigning the words in the text to various categories, the investigator usually counts the words in each category in each document. In turn, these summary measures represent the intensity of concern with each category in a given document.[28] The choice of document as the logical aggregate unit of analysis, however, is only one of several possibilities. There is some evidence (Grey, Kaplan, and Lasswell, 1965; Saris-Gallhofer et al., 1978) indicating that the reliability of content categories varies by the level of aggregation: In a comparison of hand- and computer-coded content analysis of the same texts, sentences and documents had the highest reliabilities, whereas the reliability for paragraphs was slightly lower. In addition, the reliability at all levels of aggregation was substantially less than the reliabilities for specific words or phrases.

Using people to code *New York Times* editorials that appeared during the Second World War, Grey et al. (1965) found that the substantive conclusions were affected by the type of recording unit. They coded a sample of editorials using four different units of text:

- symbols, which correspond to words or short phrases
- paragraphs
- units of three sentences
- whole editorials

They also coded each unit of text as being favorable, neutral, or unfavorable toward the symbol. Controlling for the total number of each type, they found that longer coding units (paragraphs, entire editorials) produced a greater proportion of units scored favorable or unfavorable and fewer units scored neutral than did the shorter units.

These findings question long-standing practices regarding aggregation of words into larger units in both hand-coded and computer-aided content analysis. Future research should investigate the relationships among substantive conclusions, reliability, validity, and different levels of aggregation.

Concluding Remarks

Some problems of content analysis are well-known; others require further investigation (see Chapter 4). The paper by Saris-Gallhofer and her associates (1978) mentioned above remains a model of the kind of research that is required if content analysis is to be put on a more solid footing. Even though much basic research remains to be done, the accumulated results of the last 20 years suggest that, for many kinds of problems, existing techniques of content analysis lead to valid and theoretically interesting results. Many of these techniques are discussed in the next chapter.

Suggestions for Further Reading

The symposium papers edited by Gerbner, Holsti, Krippendorff, Paisley, and Stone (1969) address many methodological issues and are still valuable reading. Kelly and Stone (1975) discuss problems in distinguishing among the various senses of words with multiple meanings. They developed one solution to this problem using procedures that are sensitive to the semantic context in which each word appears. Dunphy et al. (1989) discuss the validation of the Harvard IV-4 General Inquirer dictionary.

Validity and reliability in their most general sense are discussed in Brinberg and Kidder (1982), Campbell and Stanley (1963), Carmines and Zeller (1982), Cook and Campbell (1979), Lord and Novick (1968), Zeller and Carmines (1980), and some of the papers in Blalock (1974), to cite several possibilities. The *Sociological Methodology* series, originally published by Jossey-Bass and now published by Basil Blackwell, includes many articles on validity and reliability assessment.

3. TECHNIQUES OF CONTENT ANALYSIS

Compared with human-coded or interpretive modes of text analysis, one of the most important advantages of computer-aided content analysis is that the rules for coding text are made explicit. This public nature of the coding rules yields tools for inquiry that, when applied to a variety of texts, generate formally comparable results. Over time, this comparability should lead to the cumulation of research findings.

A second major advantage of computer-aided content analysis is that, once formalized either by computer programs and/or content-coding schemes, the computer provides perfect coder reliability in the application of coding rules to text. High coder reliability then frees the investigator to concentrate on other aspects of inquiry, such as validity, interpretation, and explanation.

Even with the assistance of computers, however, a remaining difficulty is that there is too much information in texts. Their richness and detail preclude analysis without some form of data reduction. The key to content analysis — in fact, to all modes of inquiry — is choosing a strategy for information loss that yields substantially interesting and theoretically useful generalizations while reducing the amount of information analyzed and reported by the investigator.

Researchers must, of course, tailor their methods to the requirements of their research by selecting specific techniques and integrating them with other methods, substantive considerations, and theories. To aid in that selection process, this chapter presents a wide variety of techniques for analyzing text that researchers may find useful. The central focus here is on computer-based content analysis as a means of text manipulation, data reduction, and data analysis in which the word or phrase is the basic unit.[29] Several ways of manipulating text are illustrated, including word-frequency counts, key-word-in-context (KWIC) listings, concordances, classification of words into content categories, content category counts, and retrievals based on content categories and co-occurrences. Some of these procedures are also useful in analyzing human-coded text.

The most important uses of content analysis are in research designs that relate content to noncontent variables. Other more advanced approaches to content analysis use exploratory and confirmatory factor analysis to identify themes in texts. Analysis of variance and structural equation models are often used to relate these themes to other variables. For instance, this chapter discusses research indicating that the content of newspaper editorials varies according to the type of newspaper (mass or elite). Another example shows how the content of the speeches of the German Kaiser responded to changing economic conditions. These advanced examples are discussed in some detail to clarify the logic of inquiry they entail and to clarify the substantive issues addressed.

Although this chapter presents examples drawn mainly from political sociology and political science, the techniques shown here can be applied to documents from myriad sources.

Document Selection and Sampling

Although some studies use an entire population of documents, most do not. Sampling is used primarily for the sake of economy. For content analysis, three sampling populations exist:

- communication sources
- documents
- text within documents

The sampling scheme employed will depend in large part on the population to be sampled and the kind of inferences to be made from the text. Among the communication sources that might be sampled are newspapers, magazines, and authors. To draw a sample, the universe must first be identified. For example, the universe of newspapers published in America is listed in the *Ayer Directory of Publications* (1983) and more recently (from 1987 onward) in the *Gale Directory of Publications and Broadcast Media* (1989).

Investigators interested in editorial opinions in American newspapers could take a simple random sample[30] that represented the population of newspapers. Suppose empirical evidence or theory suggested, however, that editorial opinions varied by region of the country and by frequency of publication (weekly versus daily). To insure that the sample included an adequate number of weekly and daily papers in each region, the sampling design might call for stratified sampling.[31] Here, the population of newspapers would first be divided by region and frequency of publication. Each of the resulting subpopulations would then be sampled randomly. This type of sampling design ensures that the final sample contains adequate numbers of newspapers from each subpopulation, and, more importantly, that the final sample represents the universe of daily and weekly newspapers in each region.

After identifying the communication sources to be studied, the investigator may reduce the amount of text to be analyzed by sampling documents. To avoid reaching biased or erroneous conclusions, however, researchers must take into account the conditions under which the documents were produced. For instance, consider a sample of editorials from two newspapers published both on weekdays and on Sunday. Suppose that the sample is to represent editorials in both papers over a two-year period. Also suppose that the purpose of the study is to compare and contrast editorial concerns. The investigator should consider several factors: First, newspapers usually publish several editorials per day and generally order them by importance on the editorial page. Second, editorials may vary by day of the week, with the less serious ones coming on weekends rather than on weekdays. Also, editorial writers often take note of major holidays and the arrival of and departure of the seasons. The sampling design must control for these systematic sources of variation in editorial content. For example, one might want to analyze only the first editorial that appears in each newspaper each nonholiday of a randomly selected week within each of the 24 months covered by the study.

Editorials are short documents. For longer texts, such as speeches or books, economy may suggest that sampling be employed. Here again the investigator must consider the nature of the texts. For example, speeches such as presidential acceptance speeches, State of the Union addresses, and the British Monarch's Speech from the Throne tend to have forms or organizations that reflect the partly ritualized nature of these texts. Often there exist routine introductions and closings. Domestic and financial affairs may be addressed before foreign affairs.

Where possible, the entire text should be analyzed. This preserves the semantic coherence of texts as units. If sampling is required, however, then the investigator must consider the structure of the text. For instance, the introductory and closing sections might be excluded. Portions dealing with domestic and foreign matters might be sampled separately. If the researcher must sample text within documents, each sample should consist of one or more entire paragraphs. This preserves some degree of semantic coherence. Sentences should *not* be sampled, because analyzing sentences in isolation — even ones drawn from the same text — destroys semantic coherence, making later validation and interpretation extremely difficult, if not impossible.

Text Encoding

After selecting the documents to be analyzed, the investigator must convert the text to a format and on a medium readable by the computer (i.e., machine-readable). In the early days of computers this process was notoriously costly and error-prone. The text was encoded by punching different patterns of holes in cards to represent different letters, numbers, and special characters (e.g., dollar signs and ampersands). Often the same text was punched twice to locate errors, a process called *verification*. It was not unusual for text entry to take up a large part of a modest research budget. For example, one project took about 9 person-months to keypunch, proofread, and correct almost a half million words and punctuation marks. Today, researchers can use optical scanners that read almost any typed or printed page and then transfer the text to an electronic storage medium such as tape or disk.

Key-Word-In-Context
Lists and Concordances

One of the first things the investigator wants to know is which words appear in the text and how they actually are used. Key-word-in-context (KWIC) lists (Table 3.1) show the context in which each word appears. This information can be used in a variety of ways. First, KWIC lists draw attention to the variation or consistency in word meaning and usage.[32] Second, KWIC lists provide structured information that is helpful in determining whether the meaning of particular words is dependent on their use in certain phrases or idioms. If so, the investigator will have to analyze the phrase or idiom as a single semantic unit.

Table 3.1 presents excerpts from the KWIC listing for the word *rights* in the 1980 party platforms. The two rightmost columns in the table, the document identification field (e.g., *American Democrats 1980*) and the sentence number within each document, exist for cross-reference. The computer program used to generate the KWIC list does not deal with word endings (suffixes); consequently, suffixes remain intact. Thus retrieval of sentences with *rights* excludes sentences that contain only *right*. Note that the KWIC list shows the larger context of word usage,[33] and makes syntactical and semantic differences in usage more apparent. For instance, *rights* occurs most frequently as a noun, but there are a few occasions when it functions as an adjective, as in *equal rights amendment*.

Table 3.2 presents a KWIC list for the word *state* after a computer has distinguished among its various senses and idioms. The instructions contained in this particular dictionary permit the identification of four different senses[34] of *state*:

(text continues on page 49)

TABLE 3.1

Selected Key-Word-In-Context Records for Word *Rights*, 1980 Republican and Democratic Party Platforms

1980 Reagan Republican Platform

YOUNG PEOPLE WANT THE OPPORTUNITY TO EXERCISE THE	RIGHTS	AND RESPONSIBILITIES OF ADULTS. THE REPUBLICAN PA	AR1980 372
ACTERIZED BY THE HIGHEST REGARD FOR PROTECTING THE	RIGHTS	OF LAW-ABIDING CITIZENS, AND IS CONSISTENT WITH T	AR1980 1004
OF THEIR SCHOOL SYSTEMS. WE WILL RESPECT THE	RIGHTS	OF STATE AND LOCAL AUTHORITIES IN THE MANAGEMENT	AR1980 333
RIGHTS AND THE HELSINKI AGREEMENTS WHICH GUARANTEE	RIGHTS	SUCH AS THE FREE INTERCHANGE OF INFORMATION AND T	AR1980 1391
UALLY AND STEADFASTLY COMMITTED TO THE EQUALITY OF	RIGHTS	FOR ALL CITIZENS, REGARDLESS OF RACE. AS THE PART	AR1980 206
S ISSUES, IS ULTIMATELY CONCERNED WITH EQUALITY OF	RIGHTS	UNDER THE LAW. THERE CAN BE NO DOUBT THAT THE QUE	AR1980 284
SE WHO SUPPORT OR OPPOSE RATIFICATION OF THE EQUAL	RIGHTS	AMENDMENT. WE ACKNOWLEDGE THE LEGITIMATE EFFORTS	AR1980 227
SSION ARE IN THE COURTS. RATIFICATION OF THE EQUAL	RIGHTS	AMENDMENT IS NOW IN THE HANDS OF STATE LEGISLATUR	AR1980 232
REAFFIRM OUR PARTY'S HISTORIC COMMITMENT TO EQUAL	RIGHTS	AND EQUALITY FOR WOMEN. WE	AR1980 228
XEMPTION FROM THE MILITARY DRAFT. WE SUPPORT EQUAL	RIGHTS	AND EQUAL OPPORTUNITIES FOR WOMEN, WITHOUT TAKING	AR1980 229
ON POLICY MUST BE BASED ON THE PRIMACY OF PARENTAL	RIGHTS	AND RESPONSIBILITY. FEDERAL EDUCATI	AR1980 322
N'S COMMITMENT TO DEFEND THEM.	RIGHTS	AND SOCIETAL VALUES ARE ONLY AS STRONG AS A NATIO	AR1980 152
MULTIRACIAL SOCIETY WITH GUARANTEES OF INDIVIDUAL	RIGHTS	IS POSSIBLE AND CAN WORK. REPUBLICANS BELIEVE THA	AR1980 1557
VE ECONOMIC SECURITY. HISPANICS SEEK ONLY THE FULL	RIGHTS	OF CITIZENSHIP -- IN EDUCATION, IN LAW ENFORCEMEN	AR1980 213
UNITIES FOR WOMEN, WITHOUT TAKING AWAY TRADITIONAL	RIGHTS	OF WOMEN SUCH AS EXEMPTION FROM THE MILITARY DRAF	AR1980 229
ING STRONG, EFFECTIVE ENFORCEMENT OF FEDERAL CIVIL	RIGHTS	STATUTES, ESPECIALLY THOSE DE DURING THE NEXT FOU	AR1980 209
CARE IS DEREGULATION AND AN EMPHASIS UPON CONSUMER	RIGHTS	AND PATIENT CHOICE. THE PRESCRIPTION FOR GOOD HEA	AR1980 350
IMPLEMENT THE UNITED NATIONS DECLARATION ON HUMAN	RIGHTS	AND THE HELSINKI AGREEMENTS WHICH GUARANTEE RIGHT	AR1980 1391
THEIR EMIGRATION IS A FUNDAMENTAL AFFRONT TO HUMAN	RIGHTS	AND THE U.N THE DECLINE IN EXIT VISAS TO SOVIET J	AR1980 1394
BEEN DURING THE CARTER ADMINISTRATION.	RIGHTS	IN THE SOVIET UNION WILL NOT BE IGNORED AS IT HAS	AR1980 1398
N'S RHETORIC, THE MOST FLAGRANT OFFENDERS OF HUMAN	RIGHTS	INCLUDING THE SOVIET UNION, VIETNAM, AND CUBA HAV	AR1980 1072
NS LINKED TO ITS UNDIFFERENTIATED CHARGES OF HUMAN	RIGHTS	VIOLATIONS. YET, THE CARTER ADMINISTRATION'S POLI	AR1980 1473

(continued)

TABLE 3.1 Continued

1980 Carter Democratic Platform

FAIR SHARE OF OUR ECONOMY. WE PLEDGE TO SECURE THE	RIGHTS	OF WORKING WOMEN, HOMEMAKERS, MINORITY WOMEN AND	AD1980	255
CH ARE IN OUR CURRENT LAWS IN ORDER TO VIOLATE THE	RIGHTS	OF THOSE ATTEMPTING TO ORGANIZE. WE CAN NO LONGER	AD1980	194
AS THAT EFFORT PROCEEDS, WE MUST ENSURE THAT THE	RIGHTS	OF WORKERS TO ENGAGE IN PEACEFUL PICKETING DURING	AD1980	1042
EPENDENT CONSUMER PROTECTION AGENCY.' TO PROTECT THE	RIGHTS	AND INTERESTS OF CONSUMERS. WE PLEDGE CONTINUED S	AD1980	301
EMPHASIZED THE INTENT OF CONGRESS.' 'TO PROTECT THE	RIGHTS	OF STATE AND LOCAL GOVERNMENTS AND PUBLIC AND PRI	AD1980	579
MENT OF THE CYPRUS PROBLEM BASED ON THE LEGITIMATE	RIGHTS	OF THE TWO COMMUNITIES. WE AGREE WITH SECRETARY G	AD1980	1627
H MANY AMERICANS HAVE ABOUT ABORTION. REPRODUCTIVE	RIGHTS	-- WE FULLY RECOGNIZE THE RELIGIOUS AND ETHICAL C	AD1980	374
UILDING TRADES WORKERS THE SAME PEACEFUL PICKETING	RIGHTS	CURRENTLY AFFORDED INDUSTRIAL WORKERS. LEGISLATIO	AD1980	203
ORTS. BOTH THE ERA AND DISTRICT OF COLUMBIA VOTING	RIGHTS	AMENDMENTS TO THE CONSTITUTION MUST BE RATIFIED A	AD1980	858
ST ENFORCE VIGOROUSLY THE AMENDMENTS TO THE VOTING	RIGHTS	ACT OF 1975 TO ASSIST HISPANIC CITIZENS. TO END D	AD1980	861
TO BARGAIN COLLECTIVELY, WHILE ENSURING THE LEGAL	RIGHTS	OF FARMERS. FARM LABOR--WE MUST VIGOROUSLY ENFORC	AD1980	1286
TION TO RESPECT FULLY THE HUMAN AND CONSTITUTIONAL	RIGHTS	OF ALL WITHIN OUR BORDERS. THE DEMOCRATIC PARTY A	AD1980	846
E TO THAT NEW HORIZON IS RATIFICATION OF THE EQUAL	RIGHTS	AMENDMENT.	AD1980	819
	RIGHTS	AMENDMENT.	AD1980	809
ING, EDUCATION, WELFARE AND SOCIAL SERVICES. CIVIL	RIGHTS,	AND CARE FOR THE DISABLED, ELDERLY AND VETERANS,	AD1980	335
S OF GOVERNMENT, WITH FULL PROTECTION FOR THE CIVIL	RIGHTS	AND LIBERTIES OF AMERICAN CITIZENS LIVING AT HOME	AD1980	873
THE FAIR HOUSING ACT AND TITLE VI OF THE CIVIL	RIGHTS	ACT MUST BE AMENDED TO INCLUDE THE HANDICAPPED.	AD1980	901
NITY PROGRAMS, TITLE VI AND TITLE VI OF THE CIVIL	RIGHTS	ACT, THE FAIR HOUSING LAWS, AND AFFIRMATIVE ACTIO	AD1980	834
N INVESTIGATION AND PROSECUTION OF SUSPECTED CIVIL	RIGHTS	VIOLATIONS. ATTORNEYS' OFFICES, AND SWIF	AD1980	1060
ONVENTION AND THE INTERNATIONAL COVENANTS ON HUMAN	RIGHTS	AS SOON AS POSSIBLE. WE SUPPORT SENATE RATIFICATI	AD1980	1529
D GUARANTEE FULL PROTECTION OF THE CIVIL AND HUMAN	RIGHTS	OF ALL WORKERS. WE MUST RECOGNIZE THE VALUE OF CU	AD1980	862
TIONS, WE WILL ACTIVELY PROMOTE THE CAUSE OF HUMAN	RIGHTS	AND EXPRESS AMERICA'S ABHORRENCE OF THE DENIAL OF	AD1980	1732
DING SOUTH AFRICA. WE MUST BE VIGILANT ABOUT HUMAN	RIGHTS	VIOLATIONS IN ANY COUNTRY IN WHICH THEY OCCUR INC	AD1980	1527
GROUPS, ASSERT OUR SUPPORT OF THE COURAGEOUS HUMAN	RIGHTS	ADVOCATE, NOBEL PEACE PRIZE WINNER, DR. WE SALUTE	AD1980	1478
ETWEEN OUR TWO COUNTRIES. WE WILL PURSUE OUR HUMAN	RIGHTS	CONCERNS AS A NECESSARY PART OF OVERALL PROGRESS	AD1980	1474
980 IS NOT ONLY IDENTIFIED WITH THE CAUSE OF HUMAN	RIGHTS	AND DEMOCRACY, BUT ALSO WE HAVE OPENED A NEW CHAP	AD1980	1748
LEGISLATION DESIGNED TO GIVE PROTECTION AND HUMAN	RIGHTS	TO THOSE WORKERS AFFECTED BY PLANT CLOSINGS. WE S	AD1980	208
ON OF UNIVERSALLY RECOGNIZED AND FUNDAMENTAL HUMAN	RIGHTS	THROUGHOUT THE AMERICAS BY URGING THAT THE SENATE	AD1980	1758
EXCEPT FOR CLEARLY HUMANITARIAN PURPOSES TO HUMAN	RIGHTS	VIOLATORS. WE WILL UPHOLD OUR OWN LAW AND TERMINA	AD1980	1760

TABLE 3.2

Selected Key-Word-In-Context Records for Word *State*, 1980 Republican and Democratic Party Platforms, Disambiguated Text

1980 Reagan Republican Platform

Left context	Keyword	Right context	Source	No.
ERNMENT OF NICARAGUA . WE DO2 NOT SUPPORT1 UNITE2D	STATES	ASSISTANCE TO2 ANY1 MARXIST GOVERNMENT IN THIS1 H	AR1980	1423
NOW . WE HAVE2 TO1 PUT1 THE UNITE2D	STATES	BACK1 ON THE WORLD EXPORT1 MAP	AR1980	1535
NUCLEAR POWER1 WOULD OVERTAKE THAT2 OF THE UNITE2D	STATES	BY THE EARLY1 1980 S , THREATENING THE SURVIVAL O	AR1980	1099
STRENGTH . REPUBLICANS BELIEVE1 THAT1 THE UNITE2D	STATES	CAN ONLY2 NEGOTIATE WITH THE SOVIET UNION3 FROM A	AR1980	1329
ND EVENTUALLY A MILITARY CATASTROPHY . THE UNITE2D	STATES	CANNOT ABDICATE THAT1 ROLE WITHOUT INDUCING A DI	AR1980	1113
UTION TO2 THE PROBLEM OF INEQUALITY OF THE UNITE2D	STATES	CITIZENS OF PUERTO RICO WITHIN THE FRAMEWORK OF T	AR1980	295
AT1 THE MOST1 EFFECTIVE WEAPONS AGAINST CRIME ARE1	STATE1	AND LOCAL AGENCIES . ALTHOUGH WE RECOGNIZE THE V	AR1980	533
FAMILYIES ; INTOLERABLE PRESSURE1S WILL1 BUILD1 ON	STATE1	, LOCAL AND FEDERAL BUDGETS AS1 TAX1 REVENUES D	AR1980	504
OF TURN3ING THE POOR5 INTO PERMANENT WARDS OF THE	STATE1	, TRADE2ING THEIR POLITICAL SUPPORT2 FOR CONTINUE	AR1980	213
CIAL1 WELFARE2 AGENCYIES AND STRENGTHEN1 LOCAL AND	STATE1	ADMINISTRATIVE FUNCTION2S AND - BETTER3 COORDIN	AR1980	148
ADMITITED INTO THE UNION1 AS1 A FULLLY SOVEREIGN1	STATE1	AFTER1 THEY FREE3LY SO1 DETERMINE1 . THE REPUBLIC	AR1980	294
EQUAL1 RIGHT1S AMENDMENT IS1 NOW IN THE HAND1S OF	STATE1	LEGISLATURES , AND THE ISSUE3S OF THE TIME1 EXTEN	AR1980	246
WLEDGE THE FUNDAMENTAL RIGHT2 TO2 EXISTENCE OF THE	STATE1	OF ISRAEL IS1 WRONG1 . THE IMPUTATION OF LEGITIMA	AR1980	1397
1 . WE BELIEVE1 THE ESTABLISHMENT OF A PALESTINIAN	STATE1	ON THE WEST BANK2 WOULD BE2 DESTABILIZING AND HAR	AR1980	1399
E1 GOVERNMENTS WHICH WILL1 NOT DESTROY TRADITIONAL	STATE1	SUPREMACY IN WATER1 LAW . WE MUST1 DEVELOP A PART	AR1980	774
1 A STATE1 . THIS1 ENACTMENT WILL1 ENABLE THE NEW1	STATE1	OF PUERTO RICO TO1 STAND1 ECONOMICALLY ON AN EQUA	AR1980	299
AND EFFORTS1 TO1 RETURN1 DECISION-MAKING POWER1 TO1	STATE1	AND LOCAL ELECT1ED OFFICIAL1S . WE PLEDGE TO1 REV	AR1980	1021
LP2 RETURN1 CONTROL1 OF WELFARE2 PROGRAM1S TO2 THE	STATE1S	. WE SUPPORT1 A BLOCK1 GRANT2 PROGRAM1 THAT2 WIL	AR1980	151
SUE CLOSE1 TIE3S AND FRIENDSHIP WITH MODERATE ARAB	STATE1S	. WHILE2 REEMPHASIZING OUR COMMITMENT TO2 ISRAEL	AR1980	1411
L4LING INFLUENCE1 OVER2 THE REGIONS' RESOURCE-RICH	STATE1S	, AND THEREBY TO1 GAIN1 DECISIVE POLITICAL AND E	AR1980	1391
AS3 LEFT3 , THE U.S. ARMED1 FORCE2S AT1 THEIR LOWEST	STATE2	OF PREPAREDNESS SINCE1 1950 . SERIOUSLY COMPROMIS	AR1980	1249
OPMENT . . . . IN OUR PLATFORM1 FOUR YEAR1S AGO , WE	STATE3D	THAT2 ' . THE GROWTH OF CIVILIAN NUCLEAR TECHN	AR1980	1319
US TO1 CATCH4 UP . THE SECRETARY2 OF DEFENSE HAS3	STATE3D	THAT3 EVEN5 . IF WE WERE1 TO1 MAINTAIN1 A CONSTANT	AR1980	1151
THE MINIMUM QUANTITYIES THE ARMED1 SERVICE1S HAVE3	STATE3D	THEY NEED1 . YET3 FUNDING REQUEST1S FOR SUFFICI	AR1980	1248

(continued)

47

TABLE 3.2 Continued

1980 Carter Democratic Platform

Left context	Keyword	Right context	Source	Line
NCENTIVES TO1 MAKE1 ALL1 RESIDENCES IN THE UNITE2D	STATES	ENERGY EFFICIENT , THROUGH2 UPGRADED INSULATION	AD1980	1195
ATION OF THE LEADERSHIP ROLE TAKEN1 BY THE UNITE2D	STATES	IN THE AREA OF HUMAN RIGHT1S AND URGE1 THAT1 THE	AD1980	1576
RE . WITH THOSE1 TREATYIES RATIFYIED , THE UNITE2D	STATES	IN 1980 IS1 NOT ONLY2 IDENTIFYIED WITH THE CAUSE3	AD1980	1762
AL REGIME IN THE WEST BANK2 AND GAZA , THE UNITE2D	STATES	IS1 A FULL1 PARTNER IN NEGOTIATIONS BETWEEN ISRAE	AD1980	1620
COLLECTIVE DEFENSE EFFORTS . IN 1977 , THE UNITE2D	STATES	JOIN2ED WITH NATO TO1 DEVELOP , FOR THE FIRST1 TI	AD1980	1455
2 TERM1S IN THE LAST1 THREE YEARS . THE UNITE2D	STATES	NON-FARM EXPORT1S HAVE3 RISEN1 50 PERCENT IN REAL	AD1980	157
AN ASSAULT1 ON THE VITAL INTEREST1S OF THE UNITE2D	STATES	OF AMERICA AND SUCH1 AN ASSAULT1 WILL1 BE3 REPELL	AD1980	1495
ASSISTANCE . IT IS1 UNACCEPTABLE THAT1 THE UNITE2D	STATES	RANKS 13TH AMONG 17 MAJOR1 INDUSTRIAL POWER1S IN	AD1980	1733
DING TO1 FERMENT IN THE THIRD1 WORLD . THE UNITE2D	STATES	SHOULD BE1 A POSITIVE FORCE1 FOR PEACEFUL CHANGE2	AD1980	1437
PORT1S AND REDRESS TRADE1 IMBALANCES . THE UNITE2D	STATES	SHOULD CONFORM WITH THE PRACTICE2S OF OTHER1 MAJO	AD1980	1029
18-YEAR-OLD S`IS3 INTENDED TO1 ENABLE THE UNITE2D	STATES	TO1 MOBILIZE MORE RAPID2LY IN THE EVENT3 OF AN EM	AD1980	1483
N3 STRENGTHEN1ED . AT THE SAME TIME1, THE UNITE2D	STATES'	COMMITMENT TO2 THE INDEPENDENCE , SECURITY1, AN	AD1980	1622
OME COUNTRY1IES . WE WILL1 CONTRIBUTE1 THE UNITE2D	STATES'	FAIR5 SHARE1 TO2 THE CAPITAL OF THE MULTILATERAL	AD1980	1736
WE OPPOSE1 CREATION OF AN INDEPENDENT PALESTINIAN	STATE1	- MORE THAN $10 BILLION - HAS3 BEEN3 REQUEST2ED D	AD1980	1630
D1 TO2 ISRAEL1 SINCE1 ITS CREATION AS1 A SOVEREIGN1	STATE1	AND LOCAL GOVERNMENT , REPRESENTATIVE1S OF LABOR2	AD1980	1623
ICH ACTIVELY INVOLVE3D THE ELECT2ED OFFICIALS OF	STATE1	AND COMMUNITY GROUPS' , AND AMENDMENTS TO2 THE	AD1980	783
TION AND TREATMENT ACT1 WHICH PROVIDE1S FUND1S TO1	STATE1	AND LOCAL GOVERNMENTS , THE FEDERAL GOVERNMENT WI	AD1980	982
F PROVIDE1ING IMMEDIATE1 FEDERAL FISCAL RELIEF TO1	STATE1	AND LOCAL GOVERNMENTS FOR THEIR WELFARE2 COST1S A	AD1980	550
HE OPPOSITE - TO1 PROVIDE1 GREAT3ER ASSISTANCE TO1	STATE1	AND LOCAL GOVERNMENT IN SETTING POLICY AND IN RE	AD1980	569
FICANT ADMINISTRATIVE AND ORGANIZATIONAL ROLES FOR	STATE1	IN PURSUEING HUMAN RIGHT1S , DEMOCRACY , AND ECO	AD1980	371
HE REGION . WE WILL1 JOIN2 WITH OTHER1 LIKE-MINDED	STATE1	IN THE PACIFIC1 BASIN PLAY2 IN THE SOLIDIFICATIO	AD1980	1775
HE U. S. TERRITORYIES AND OTHER1 EMERGE1ING ISLAND	STATE1	IN THE REGION TO1 SUPPORT1 THE HISTORIC EFFORTS	AD1980	1801
BUILD1 A COMPREHENSIVE PEACE1 . WE CALL1 UPON ALL1	STATE1	NOT PROVIDE1ING ASSISTANCE TO2 UNIFYIED FAMILYIE	AD1980	1639
M OUR SUPPORT2 FOR THE 1962 ACTION AND URGE1 THAT1	STATE1		AD1980	562
NATIONAL ECONOMIC1 PROSPERITY . OUR 1976 PLATFORM1	STATE3D	; EVEN2 DURING PERIODS OF NORMAL ECONOMIC1 GROWT	AD1980	129
ITS HOLY PLACE1S PROVIDE1D TO2 ALL1 FAITH1S . AS1	STATE3D	IN THE 1976 PLATFORM2 , THE DEMOCRATIC PARTY2 RE	AD1980	1635
OUS TO2 A BEAUTIFUL MOSAIC . PRESIDENT CARTER HAS3	STATE3D	THAT1 THE COMPOSITION OF AMERICAN1 SOCIETY IS1 A	AD1980	1008

- state (noun; body politic or area of government)
- situation (e.g., *state of science*)
- to state (verb; to declare)
- "united states" (idiom; handled by the second sense of *United*)

A KWIC list can be thought of as a concordance, a listing by word of each word in the text together with its context (Burton, 1981, 1982; Hockey and Marriott, 1982; Hockey and Martin, 1987; Preston and Coleman, 1978). Often used in literary or biblical studies, concordances provide a rich data base for detailed studies of word usage in all kinds of texts. For example, the KWIC lists shown in Tables 3.1 and 3.2 illustrate excerpts from a much larger KWIC list for party platforms from 1968 to 1980. This larger data base can be used to study detailed differences and similarities in symbol usage in party platforms from this period.

Concordances do not automatically show the referents of pronouns and ambiguous phrases. Furthermore, unlike retrievals from text based on category assignments (which are discussed later in this chapter) concordances do not organize the text according to synonyms or words with similar connotations. A concordance or KWIC list with sentence identification numbers, however, makes it easy for the investigator to examine a sentence in its larger textual context. This examination often will reveal synonyms or pronouns that need to be taken into account.

Although concordances and KWIC lists provide essential information concerning symbol usage, they are, at least initially, data-expanding rather than data-reducing techniques. If the concordance presents each word with three words to the left or the right, for example, the original text is expanded by a factor of six. How, then, can investigators narrow their focus? Concordances lend themselves to the intensive study of a few specific symbols, such as *equal rights amendment* or *women*. Consequently, investigators will have to translate substantive hypotheses into concern with specific symbols.

Word-Frequency Lists

Researchers can view texts from another perspective by examining the highest-frequency words. Because each accounts for a relatively large proportion of the text, many content analysts focus their efforts primarily on the most frequently occurring words. Table 3.3 presents ordered word-frequency lists for the 1976 and 1980 Democratic and

TABLE 3.3

Ordered Word-Frequency Lists,
1976-1980 Democratic and Republican Party Platforms

Jimmy Carter, 1976			Gerald Ford, 1976			Jimmy Carter, 1980			Ronald Reagan, 1980		
Rank	Word	Frequency	Rank	Word	Frequency	Rank	Word	Frequency	Rank	Word	Frequency
1	OUR	222	1	OUR	318	1	OUR	430	1	OUR	347
2	MUST	140	2	MUST	148	2	MUST	321	2	THEIR	161
3	SHOULD	130	3	SHOULD	109	3	DEMOCRATIC	226	3	ADMINISTRATION	131
4	DEMOCRATIC	90	4	GOVERNMENT	100	4	FEDERAL	177	4	GOVERNMENT	128
5	GOVERNMENT	87	5	STATES	86	5	SUPPORT	144	5	REPUBLICAN	126
6	ECONOMIC	78	6	FEDERAL	75	6	PARTY	139	5	FEDERAL	126
6	SUPPORT	78	7	UNITED	74	7	GOVERNMENT	133	6	AMERICAN	119
7	FEDERAL	74	8	SUPPORT	73	8	PROGRAMS	129	7	REPUBLICANS	116
8	ALL	72	9	ALL	70	9	ADMINISTRATION	127	8	CARTER	112
9	STATES	69	10	THEIR	66	10	ALL	122	9	MUST	104
9	UNITED	69	11	NATIONAL	61	10	ECONOMIC	122	10	ECONOMIC	101
10	POLICY	67	12	POLICY	60	11	THEIR	112	11	POLICY	100
10	PROGRAMS	67	13	AMERICAN	56	12	CONTINUE	109	12	SOVIET	98
11	PARTY	66	14	PROGRAMS	52	13	ENERGY	107	13	STATES	93
12	ENERGY	62	15	REPUBLICAN	51	14	SHOULD	99	14	MILITARY	89
13	NATIONAL	59	16	PEOPLE	49	15	OTHER	96	15	TAX	85
14	PUBLIC	51	17	CONGRESS	48	16	POLICY	89	16	SUPPORT	83
15	AMERICAN	48	19	WORLD	46	17	EFFORTS	87	17	ENERGY	81
16	PEOPLE	47	19	MORE	45	17	DEVELOPMENT	87	17	MORE	81
17	THEIR	46	20	SYSTEM	44	18	RIGHTS	86	18	PARTY	79
18	HEALTH	45	21	DEMOCRATIC	43	19	HEALTH	85	19	PEOPLE	74
19	OTHER	44	22	DEVELOPMENT	42	20	AMERICAN	84	20	UNITED	73
20	INTERNATIONAL	43	23	ECONOMIC	41	21	PROGRAM	81	21	THEY	72
21	DEVELOPMENT	42	23	ENERGY	41	21	MORE	81	22	ALL	70
22	NEEDS	40	23	OTHER	41	22	NATIONAL	80	22	POLICIES	70
23	POLICIES	39	24	THEY	40	23	NEW	79	23	AMERICANS	68
23	TAX	39	25	NEW	39	24	STATES	73	24	SHOULD	64
24	MORE	38	26	CONTINUE	37	25	SECURITY	72	25	NEW	63
24	SYSTEM	38	27	THROUGH	36	26	WOMEN	70	26	BELIEVE	62
25	NEW	37	28	LOCAL	35	27	WORK	69	26	DEFENSE	62
26	ADMINISTRATION	36	29	AMERICANS	33	28	EDUCATION	65	26	NATIONAL	62
26	EFFORTS	36	29	NATIONS	33	29	YEARS	64	26	WHO	62
26	WORLD	36	29	TAX	33	30	NEEDS	62	27	PLEDGE	61
27	HOUSING	34	30	WORK	32	30	PEOPLE	62	28	FOREIGN	60
28	FULL	33	31	CARE	30	31	ALSO	61	29	GROWTH	58
29	CITIZENS	32	31	FOREIGN	30	32	THEY	60	30	OTHER	55
30	BOTH	31	31	MOST	30	32	WORLD	60	31	MOST	53
30	FORCES	31	31	NOW	30	33	SOVIET	58	31	SECURITY	53
30	RIGHTS	31	31	SECURITY	30	34	HUMAN	57	32	YEARS	51
30	AREAS	30	32	RESOURCES	30	35	PROVIDE	56	33	THROUGH	50
31	PROVIDE	30	32	THERE	29	35	UNITED	56	34	INFLATION	49
31	SOCIAL	30	32	USE	29	36	INTERNATIONAL	55	34	PRIVATE	49
31	WORK	30	33	RIGHTS	28	36	AREAS	55	35	JOBS	48
31	YEARS	30	33	SHALL	28	36	CARE	55			

Republican party platforms.[35] Three aspects of this table deserve mention. First, the computer program that generated these lists was instructed to omit certain frequently occurring words that are usually substantively uninteresting; for example, articles such as *a* and *the,* and forms of the verb *to be* such as *is* and *was.*[36] These words, however, could easily have been included. The program also omitted one- and two-letter words, such as *I* and *we.* Second, as with the KWIC lists, the computer program used to generate word frequencies does not deal with word endings (suffixes). Consequently, *Republican* and *Republicans* appear as separate entries. Third, there are many more low-frequency than high-frequency words. In the 1980 Republican Platform, for example, there are 4619 different word forms, of which 2307 — or slightly less than half — occur only once (data not shown). This large proportion of infrequently occurring word forms is found in all naturally occurring texts, that is, those not conducted for special purposes such as linguistic analysis (Zipf, 1932, 1965). Analyzing the many low-frequency words is not very efficient, and, as noted, researchers often focus their attention on the fewer high-frequency words.

Examining the list for the 1976 platforms suggests that the Carter and Ford documents used similar words with about the same relative frequencies. For example, the two most frequent words in each platform are identical, and there are obvious similarities in the top 10 words. Nevertheless, noticeable differences exist. *Economic* and *health* are ranked 6th and 18th in the Carter platform, whereas in the Ford platform *economic* ranks only 23rd and *health* is not among the most frequent words.

Comparison of the 1976 with the 1980 platforms reveals striking differences. *Soviet, military,* and *defense* rank high in Reagan's platform but are not among the most frequent words in either of the 1976 platforms. *Soviet* ranks 33rd in the 1980 Carter platform, but the other two words fail to make this short list. *Health, women,* and *education* rank high in the 1980 Carter document but are not among the high-frequency words in the Reagan document.

This table confirms that the Reagan platform articulated a very different set of priorities and concerns than either the Carter campaign, or the previous Ford Republican platform. The relationship between articulations and actions remains to be investigated thoroughly. In a great many instances, however, the Reagan platforms advocated policies that were a radical departure from the policies articulated by the Ford and Carter campaigns. Similar data can be generated over long periods of time to study the relationships among articulations, policy changes, and voter responses.

Ordered word-frequency lists provide a convenient way of getting at gross differences in word usage. Table 3.3 illustrates that these differences may be between

- the same message source at different points in time;
- different message sources at the same time; or
- both.

Several assumptions underlie this mode of analysis. An obvious one is that the most frequently appearing words reflect the greatest concerns. This is likely to be generally true, but two cautions must be noted. First, one word may be used in a variety of contexts or may have more than one meaning, so that word frequencies may suggest far greater uniformity in usage than actually exists, thus questioning the validity of inferences from word-frequency data. For instance, *states* appears frequently in all four platforms. One cannot tell from just the word-frequency list whether the platform addresses states' rights, the United States, sovereign states, or the state of affairs. To augment a word-frequency list, however, a concordance can often help the researcher to assess the uniformity of word usage and to generate counts of specific phrases.

Second, the use of synonyms and/or pronouns for stylistic reasons may lead to the underestimation of actual concern with particular words or phrases. For example, in Democratic platforms the pronoun *we* may refer to the party or to an incumbent administration. If one were interested in counting self-references, perhaps the best index would be the sum of references to *we* in the former sense (the phrase *Democratic Party*) and perhaps references to *our party*. Thus counts of any one, rather than all, of these words or phrases will yield less valid indicators of self-reference. No simple, widely available resolution of this problem currently exists, especially one for large amounts of text. Key-word-in-context lists discussed in the previous section do provide the basis for valid indicators of concepts such as party self-reference. For studies using numerous indicators, however, this may be an impractical, time-consuming answer.[37]

The previous chapter noted the ability of some computer software to distinguish among words with more than one meaning or to treat phrases as a single semantic unit. Table 3.4 presents ordered word-frequency lists for the 1976 and 1980 party platforms based on disambiguated text. *Support,* for example, moves from 5th to 23rd and 25th in the 1980 Carter platform. The first sense of *support* is the verb form; the second sense is the noun form, meaning sustain, provide for, or encouragement, as in *The bill has our support.* The ranking of most words, however, does not change greatly. Consequently, the overall conclusions would not be very different because of disambiguation. Nevertheless, because this text classification procedure is more precise, the data in Table 3.4 have greater semantic validity than the data in the previous table.

Although word-frequency lists reveal changes or differences in emphasis between documents, they must be used with caution. Word frequencies do not reveal very much about the associations among words. For example, although it may be interesting to know that *support* ranks higher in the 1980 Carter than in the 1980 Reagan platform, one cannot tell whether the platforms differ in their support of democratic

TABLE 3.4

Ordered Word-Frequency Lists,
1976-1980 Democratic and Republican Party Platforms,
Disambiguated Text

Jimmy Carter, 1976			Gerald Ford, 1976			Jimmy Carter, 1980			Ronald Reagan, 1980		
Rank	Word	Frequency	Rank	Word	Frequency	Rank	Word	Frequency	Rank	Word	Frequency
1	OUR	222	1	OUR	318	1	OUR	430	1	OUR	347
2	MUST1	140	2	MUST1	148	2	MUST1	321	2	THEIR	161
3	SHOULD	130	3	SHOULD	109	3	DEMOCRATIC	226	3	GOVERNMENT	128
4	DEMOCRATIC	90	4	GOVERNMENT	100	4	FEDERAL	177	4	FEDERAL	126
5	GOVERNMENT	87	5	FEDERAL	75	5	GOVERNMENT	133	4	REPUBLICAN	126
6	ECONOMIC1	78	6	THEIR	67	6	PROGRAM1S	129	5	ADMINISTRATION1	125
7	FEDERAL	74	7	STATES	65	7	ADMINISTRATION1	124	6	AMERICAN1	117
8	POLICY	67	7	UNITE2D	65	8	ECONOMIC1	122	7	REPUBLICANS	116
8	PROGRAM1S	67	8	NATIONAL	61	9	PARTY2	116	8	CARTER	112
9	PARTY1	66	9	POLICY	60	10	THEIR	112	9	MUST1	104
10	ENERGY	62	10	AMERICAN1	56	11	CONTINUE1	109	10	ECONOMIC1	101
11	ALL1	59	11	ALL1	53	12	ENERGY	107	11	POLICY	100
11	NATIONAL	59	12	PROGRAM1S	52	13	ALL1	106	12	SOVIET	98
12	UNITE2D	55	13	REPUBLICAN	51	14	SHOULD	99	13	MILITARY	89
13	STATES	54	14	PEOPLE1	49	15	OTHER1	96	14	ENERGY	81
14	PEOPLE1	47	15	WORLD	46	16	POLICY	89	14	MORE	81
15	AMERICAN1	46	16	MORE	45	17	DEVELOPMENT	87	15	TAX1	80
15	THEIR	46	16	SUPPORT1	45	17	EFFORTS	87	16	PEOPLE1	74
16	HEALTH	45	17	SYSTEM	44	18	HEALTH	85	17	PROGRAM1S	73
17	PUBLIC1	44	18	DEVELOPMENT	43	19	AMERICAN1	84	18	THEY	72
18	INTERNATIONAL1	43	19	DEMOCRATIC	43	19	MORE	81	19	POLICYIES	70
19	DEVELOPMENT	42	20	ECONOMIC1	41	20	PROGRAM1	81	20	UNITE2D	69
19	OTHER	42	20	ENERGY	41	21	NATIONAL	80	21	AMERICAN1S	68
20	SUPPORT1	41	21	THEY	40	22	NEW1	79	22	STATES	67
21	POLICYIES	39	22	CONGRESS1	38	23	SUPPORT1	75	23	SHOULD	64
22	MORE	38	22	NEW1	38	24	WOMEN	72	24	DEFENSE	64
22	SYSTEM	38	23	CONTINUE1	37	25	SUPPORT2	71	24	NEW1	62
22	THESE1	38	23	OTHER1	37	26	EDUCATION	65	24	NATIONAL	62
22	TAX1	38	24	LOCAL	35	26	RIGHT1S	65	24	WHO	62
23	SUPPORT2	37	25	AMERICAN1S	33	27	YEAR1S	64	25	BELIEVE1	61
23	NEW1	37	25	NATIONS	33	28	PEOPLE1	62	25	PLEDGE	61
24	EFFORTS	36	26	TAX1	31	29	ALSO	61	26	FOREIGN1	60
24	WORLD	36	27	FOREIGN1	30	30	THEY	60	27	ALL1	59
25	HOUSE4ING	34	27	NOW	30	30	WORLD	60	28	GROWTH	58
26	FULL1	33	28	RESOURCES	29	31	SOVIET	58	29	PARTY3	56
26	ADMINISTRATION1	33	28	THROUGH2	29	32	HUMAN	57	30	MOST1	51
27	CITIZENS	32	29	RIGHT1S	28	33	PROVIDE1	56	31	OTHER1	50
28	AREAS	30	29	SUPPORT2	28	34	AREAS	55	31	SUPPORT1	50
28	NEED2S	30	30	INTERNATIONAL1	27	34	CARE1	55	32	INFLATION	49
28	YEAR1S	30	31	COMMUNITY	26	34	INTERNATIONAL1	55	32	PRIVATE1	49
28	PROVIDE1	30	31	HEALTH	26	34	PERCENT	55	33	JOBS	48
28	EMPLOYMENT	30	31	PARTY1	26	35	NEED2S	54	33	PERCENT	48
29	REPUBLICAN	29	31	PROVIDE1	26	36	ASSISTANCE	51	33	SYSTEM	48
29	MILITARY	29	32	NATION	25	36	RESOURCES	51			

principles, of the equal rights amendment, or of foreign countries that have pro-Western authoritarian regimes. Having used ordered word-frequency lists to identify words of potential interest, the investigator should use KWIC lists for retrievals from text to test hypotheses concerning the larger context of symbol usage.

Retrievals from Coded Text

With computer-aided content analysis, the investigator easily may search through the text to retrieve portions meeting specific criteria (see Ogilvie, 1966; Stone, Dunphy, Smith, and Ogilvie, 1966: 121ff). One way of searching text is to retrieve sentences by the occurrence of at least one word in a particular category, for example, all sentences with one WEALTH word. Some investigators (DeWeese, personal communication) strongly feel that counts and retrievals based on the co-occurrence[38] or combination of categories or words in a single sentence are the most useful indicators. Of course, one difficulty is knowing in advance which combinations will be particularly useful. Presumably, substantive hypotheses suggest appropriate combinations, but induction usually prevails in these instances. Another difficulty in analyzing co-occurrences is that infrequently occurring combinations might be of substantive interest, for example, references to *individual rights,* which occurred only twice in the 1980 Reagan platform and not at all in the 1980 Carter platform (Table 3.1). In the social science literature there is little, if any, systematic research on retrievals; hence, only a brief example will be given.

Using party platforms 1844-1864, the computer was instructed to retrieve all sentences with at least one WEALTH word that was a noun and that also had any word in the category WELL-BEING-DEPRIVATION. The latter category indicates a concern with the loss of well-being, either of a person or a collectivity. Table 3.5 presents a sample of nine sentences meeting this criterion.[39] The criterion words are underscored. The program retrieved sentences addressing two different subjects. Some sentences mention economic difficulties; others mention pensions for the survivors of the war dead and for the disabled. The third sentence in the table contains both themes.

Obviously, the diversity of sentences retrieved can be narrowed or expanded by varying the criteria of selection: more criteria will result in fewer retrievals, and fewer criteria will result in more. But the primary difficulty is that the results depend on an interaction among the text, the category scheme, and the assignment of words to categories. Thus each investigator will have to experiment with retrievals to find the most helpful approach. No general guidelines now exist.

Finally, why use retrievals based on categories? Why not use retrievals based on words? Certainly the computer is capable of doing either. For example, one could retrieve all sentences containing the words *pension* or *pensions.* This might retrieve some sentences, however, dealing with the pensions of postal workers. Instead, sentences with *pension* and *disability* could be retrieved, but this would miss the second sentence in Table 3.5, which is similar in content to the others dealing with pensions for veterans and their survivors. Synonyms frequently are used that would be missed by a purely word-oriented approach to retrievals, but they are captured more easily in a category-based system.

TABLE 3.5

Selected Retrievals, Democratic and Republican Platforms: Sentences with WEALTH Nouns and WELL-BEING-DEPRIVATION, 1844-1964

```
DOC# 15   SENT# 12   ID=D1868
AND A TARIFF FOR REVENUE UPON FOREIGN1 IMPORTS , SUCH2 AS WILL2 AFFORD1 INCIDENTAL PROTECTION TO2 DOMESTIC
MANUFACTURE1S, AND AS1 WILL1 , WITHOUT IMPAIRING THE REVENUE , IMPOSE THE LEAST2 BURDEN1 UPON , AND BEST PROMOTE AND
ENCOURAGE1 THE GREAT1 INDUSTRIAL INTEREST1S OF THE COUNTRY1 .
*** END DOCUMENT. NUMBER RETRIEVALS=   1

DOC# 18   SENT# 23   ID=R1872
THEIR PENSIONS ARE1 A SACRED DEBT OF THE NATION , AND THE WIDOW1S AND ORPHANS OF THOSE2 WHO DIED FOR THEIR COUNTRY1
ARE3 ENTITLED TO2 THE CARE1 OF A GENEROUS AND GRATEFUL PEOPLE1 .
*** END DOCUMENT. NUMBER RETRIEVALS=   1

DOC# 22   SENT# 16   ID=R1880
AND THAT1 THE LIBERTY SECURE1D TO2 THIS1 GENERATION SHOULD BE3 TRANSMITTED UNDIMINISHED TO2 OTHER1 GENERATIONS , THAT1
THE ORDER2 ESTABLISHED AND THE CREDIT1 ACQUIRE2D SHOULD NEVER BE3 IMPAIRED , THAT1 THE PENSIONS PROMISE2D SHOULD BE3
PAID1 , THAT1 THE DEBT SO1 MUCH REDUCED SHOULD BE3 EXTINGUISHED BY THE FULL1 PAYMENT OF EVERY DOLLAR
*** END DOCUMENT. NUMBER RETRIEVALS=   1

DOC# 24   SENT# 31   ID=R1884
THE GRATEFUL THANK2S OF THE AMERICAN PEOPLE1 ARE1 DUE1 TO2 THE UNION1 SOLDIERS AND SAILORS OF THE LATE2 WAR1 AND THE
REPUBLICAN PARTY1 STAND1S PLEDGED TO2 SUITABLE PENSIONS FOR ALL2 WHO WERE3 DISABLED , AND FOR THE WIDOW1S AND ORPHANS
OF THOSE2 WHO DIED IN THE WAR1 .
*** END DOCUMENT. NUMBER RETRIEVALS=   1

DOC# 24   SENT# 33   ID=R1884
SO2 THAT1 ALL1 INVALID SOLDIERS SHALL SHARE1 ALIKE , AND THEIR PENSIONS BEGIN1 WITH THE DATE1 OF DISABILITY OR
DISCHARGE1 , AND NOT WITH THE DATE1 OF APPLICATION .
*** END DOCUMENT. NUMBER RETRIEVALS=   2

DOC# 29   SENT# 50   ID=D1896
RECOGNIZING THE JUST3 CLAIM1S OF DESERVING UNION1 SOLDIERS , WE HEARTYLY INDORSE THE RULE1 OF THE PRESENT1
COMMISSIONER OF PENSIONS , THAT1 NOT NAME1S SHALL BE3 ARBITRARYLY DROP3PED FROM THE PENSION ROLL1 , AND THE FACT1 OF
ENLISTMENT AND SERVICE1 SHOULD BE3 DEEMED CONCLUSIVE EVIDENCE1 AGAINST DISEASE AND DISABILITY BEFORE ENLISTMENT .
*** END DOCUMENT. NUMBER RETRIEVALS=   1

DOC# 30   SENT# 21   ID=R1896
WE BELIEVE1 THE REPEAL OF THE RECIPROCITY ARRANGEMENTS NEGOTIATED BY THE LAST1 REPUBLICAN ADMINISTRATION1 WAS1 A
NATIONAL CALAMITY , AND DEMAND2 THEIR RENEWAL AND EXTENSION ON SUCH1 TERM3S AS1 WILL1 EQUALIZE OUR TRADE1 WITH OTHER1
NATIONS , REMOVE THE RESTRICTIONS WHICH NOW OBSTRUCT THE SALE OF AMERICA1 PRODUCT1S IN THE PORTS OF OTHER1 COUNTRY1IES+
*** END DOCUMENT. NUMBER RETRIEVALS=   1

DOC# 30   SENT# 35   ID=R1896
WE ARE3 UNALTERABLELY OPPOSE2D TO2 EVERY MEASURE1 CALCULATE2D TO1 DEBASE OUR CURRENCY OR IMPAIR THE CREDIT1 OF OUR
COUNTRY1 .
*** END DOCUMENT. NUMBER RETRIEVALS=   3

DOC# 31   SENT# 67   ID=D1900
WE ARE1 PROUD OF THE COURAGE AND FIDELITY OF THE AMERICAN SOLDIERS AND SAILORS IN ALL1 OUR WAR1S , WE FAVOR2 LIBERAL2
PENSIONS TO2 THEM AND THEIR DEPENDENTS , AND WE REITERATE THE POSITION1 TAKEN1 IN THE CHICAGO PLATFORM2 OF 1896
THAT1 THE FACT1 OF ENLISTMENT AND SERVICE1 SHALL BE3 DEEMED CONCLUSIVE EVIDENCE1 AGAINST DISEASE AND DISABILITY BEFORE
ENLISTMENT
*** END DOCUMENT. NUMBER RETRIEVALS=   1
```

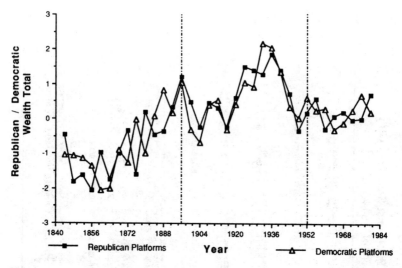

Figure 3.1. Republican and Democratic Concern with WEALTH-TOTAL, 1844-1980

Category Counts

Another approach to analyzing text counts words that have been classified into categories. As noted above, counting assumes that higher relative counts (proportions, percentages, or ranks) reflect higher concern with the category.

Counting is often useful because it may reveal aspects of the text that would not be apparent otherwise. For instance, one substantive question that arises in the analysis of party platforms is: Over time, how do the Democrats and Republicans vary with respect to each other in their concerns? Figure 3.1 shows each party's concern with WEALTH-TOTAL 1844-1980.[40] For each party, the data consist of the percentage of words in each platform categorized in WEALTH-TOTAL.[41]

Between 1844 and about 1952 there is a general rise in the percentage of each platform devoted to economic matters (Figure 3.1). This increase probably reflects greater importance of the state in the management of economic affairs. Second, from 1952 or so to the present there is a relatively constant level of concern with economic matters. Third, and more important, since 1844 the character of competition between the parties has changed qualitatively in dramatic ways.[42] From 1844 through the election of 1892 (the left vertical reference line) the parties

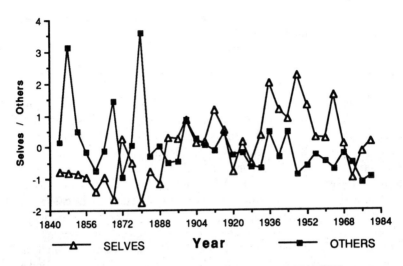

Figure 3.2. Democratic Concern with SELVES and OTHERS, 1844-1980

have varied opposite to each other in their concern with economic matters. Between 1896 and 1952 (the right vertical reference line) the parties manifest similar levels of economic concerns. Between 1952 and 1980, however, they move opposite each other again, although the overall variation in this time period is relatively small. The break points of 1894 and 1952 are congruent with Burnham's (1970) and others' interpretations of periodic realignments of the American party system (see Namenwirth and Weber, 1987: chapter 4).

Not only may simple counts reveal differences between message sources but they also may show how the communication content from one message source varies over time. From the Democratic party, Figure 3.2 illustrates how party platforms vary with respect to first-person plural pronouns (SELVES) and third person plural pronouns (OTHERS). As might be expected, these categories vary inversely with each other: When the Democrats emphasize their own accomplishments and programs, they de-emphasize those of the opposition. For Republican platforms, similar results were found (figure not shown here). Even though these examples are drawn from political sociology, comparing simple percentages has been used in other realms to great advantage. For example, Aries (1973, 1977) analyzed conversations in small groups to make inferences about sex-role differences in group interactions (see Chapter 1 for a summary).

Measurement Models

Although the preceding methods often work quite well, investigators have used a variety of multivariate data analysis techniques to analyze data based on text. One often-used technique is known as *factor analysis,*[43] a general name for several related mathematical procedures that summarize the variation of many observed or measured variables in terms of fewer underlying or latent variables that are called *factors.* The variation in these underlying factors usually is assumed to cause the variation in the observed variables. In content-analytic research, the observed variables are often categories and the factors often are assumed to be underlying themes in the text. The extent to which an observed variable is correlated to a latent variable or factor is called a *factor loading,* which is similar to a correlation coefficient. These ideas are illustrated in the following example.

This section reports some of the factor-analysis results in a study of American and British newspaper editorials (Namenwirth and Bibbee, 1975) and then considers interpretive problems. The next section outlines and critiques the substantive results based on the themes described here.

Using the General Inquiry computer system (Stone et al., 1966) and the Namenwirth Political Dictionary[44] (Namenwirth, no date), 288 randomly selected editorials concerning the Korean War from mass (*New York Daily News, Boston Daily Record,* and *Washington Daily News*) and elite (*New York Times, Christian Science Monitor,* and *Washington Post*) newspapers were classified into categories. For each editorial the computer reported the percentage of words in each of 40 categories retained for analysis.[45] Principal components analysis[46] produced four interpretable factors (accounting for 33% of the total variance). Table 3.6 presents factor loadings on the first two factors for each category. These numbers may be interpreted as the correlation between the category and the factor (loadings < .30 are omitted).

Categories that correlate (load on) with the same factor tend to vary together and investigators usually interpret them as representing a theme in the text. For example, editorials that have frequent references to American leaders and topics (AMERICAN) will also contain frequent references to words with higher status connotations (HIGHER STATUS)

TABLE 3.6

Selected Themes in Korean War Editorials in Mass and Prestige (Elite) Newspapers

Theme 1: Control of the Social Environment—Parochialism Versus Cosmopolitan

Parochialism Categories	Loadings	Cosmopolitan Categories	Loadings*
American	.85	International Institution	−.53
Higher Status	.80	Approach	−.44
Job Role	.79	Sign Accept	−.42
Male Role	.68	Danger Theme	−.34
Selves	.43	Static	−.32
Sign Authority	.55		

Theme 2: Control of the Physical Environment—Economic Versus Military

Economic Categories	Loadings	Military Categories	Loadings
Sign Authority	.68	Death Theme	−.44
Collective Static	.64	Social Place	−.33
Action Norm	.55	Natural World	−.31
Guide	.47		
Ought	.46		
Control	.45		
Ideal Value	.41		
Work	.40		
Individual Static	.39		
Collective Dynamic	.35		
Sign Accept	.35		
Economic	.31		
Technological	.30		

SOURCE: Adapted from Namenwirth and Bibbee (1975)
* Loadings < |.30| are omitted.

and occupational references (JOB ROLE). Other editorials manifest concern with INTERNATIONAL INSTITUTIONS, conciliatory feelings and moods (APPROACH), words implying interpersonal acceptance (SIGN ACCEPT), words connoting alarm or concern with danger (DANGER THEME), and words concerned with maintaining the status quo (STATIC).

What do these themes mean or signify, and how can the investigator validate their interpretation? A discussion of factor interpretation is beyond the scope of this section. Some practical guidelines, however, may be helpful. For each editorial, the factor analysis procedure computes a score for each factor or theme that indicates the extent to which the editorial reflects the factor. To determine if these themes are real rather than statistical artifacts, these steps should be taken. First, the analyst should examine those editorials that have the highest positive and the highest negative factor scores. Typically, texts with similar scores manifest similar concerns. Second, the analyst should determine how the words in these exemplary texts are classified. There should be many words classified in the categories that have high loadings on the factor. Third, the analyst should compare the texts with extreme positive and negative factor scores with each other and with texts that have scores of nearly zero for that theme (factor). These contrasts should show that texts with high positive scores are quite different in content from those with zero scores, and that they are in some sense opposite to those with high negative scores.

Furthermore, each factor can be thought of as representing a controversy of some sort. The themes at the positive and negative poles typically are opposing resolutions of the underlying controversy. Examination of editorials with extreme positive and negative scores on Factor 1 suggested to Namenwirth and Bibbee that this controversy addresses control of the social environment. Editorials propose two alternative solutions, which they label *parochial* versus *cosmopolitan.* The parochial theme "stresses a fortress America stance: nationalism and isolationism best serve American interests and world peace" (Namenwirth and Bibbee, 1975: 53), as illustrated by this excerpt from the *Boston Daily Record,* May 4, 1951, titled "Now Let Us Have Facts:"

> More than 10,500 Americans are dead in Korea because these three men [Truman, Acheson, and Marshall][47] had a vested interest in their own mistakes. . . . Our concern is our sons in Korea. We frankly do not want any more Americans to die on that Asian peninsula seven thousand miles away from our shores, to protect the synthetic reputations of Acheson and Truman. Our sole concern is America and Americans. And that, we truly believe, is the concern of 99 percent of the American people. (Namenwirth and Bibbee, 1975: 53)

The cosmopolitan theme emphasizes "the need for an active role in world affairs, urging constant diplomatic initiative, coordination, and conciliation" (Namenwirth and Bibbee, 1975: 53), as illustrated by this excerpt from the December 3, 1952, *Christian Science Monitor* editorial titled "Unity in the UN:"

> To the [anti-communists] the [communist rejection of the Indian Truce Plan] should suggest the possibility of a considerable strain between Moscow and Peking on this matter, a strain which free world diplomacy may exploit to advantage in the future. . . . It would be a great mistake for the anti-communist world to ignore the possibility [of future Chinese independence from Moscow], as it would be unrealistic for the neutral world to expect too much from it too soon. . . . Meanwhile, the precarious unity of the non-communist countries, as shown in the UN vote, can best be maintained as the United States demonstrates how far it is from seeking to dominate its friends and allies in the iron-fisted Moscow manner. (Namenwirth and Bibbee, 1975: 54)

The second issue or theme (Table 3.6) concerns contrasting approaches to control of the physical environment: Some editorials stress economic problems whereas other editorials stress military problems. Economic concerns mainly address inflation and the government's instituting and administering of a wartime system of price controls. Several categories correlate positively with this factor: normative patterns of social behavior (ACTION NORM); social/emotional actions consisting of assistance and positive direction (GUIDE); words indicating a moral imperative (OUGHT); words about limiting action (CONTROL); task activity (WORK); culturally defined virtues, goals, valued conditions, and activities (IDEAL VALUE); the ECONOMIC and TECHNOLOGICAL rules, actions, and contexts,[48] concern with the maintenance of the status quo, with the collectivity as agent or object of preferred action (COLLECTIVE STATIC); and the same as the former, but indicating a concern with the change of the status quo (COLLECTIVE DYNAMIC).

The ECONOMIC theme is illustrated by this portion of the August 16, 1950, *Washington Post* editorial titled "Defense Organization:"

> The limited authority [Truman] has requested to allocate scarce materials, give priority to defense orders, tighten credit controls, and increase taxes certainly does not require any additional control machinery. . . . For the present, the existing organizational setup seems adequate to establish effective controls over allocations of the limited number of raw materials in short supply. . . . However much we may dislike the prospect, any effective general control over prices and living costs would necessitate the creation of a huge bureaucratic agency comparable to the Office of Price Administration. The government would also need new agencies to settle labor disputes, control and adjust wages. (Namenwirth and Bibbee, 1975: 55)

Editorials manifesting the opposing theme are mainly concerned with the cost of military intervention in terms of wounded and mutilated soldiers (DEATH THEME) and military solutions for these emergencies. These problem solutions are also seen as part of nature rather than society (SOCIAL PLACE, NATURAL WORLD). The following passage, from an editorial titled "Saving the Wounded" that appears in the April 5, 1952, *New York Times,* illustrates this military theme:

> Good news from the Korean battle front was reported in a recent address in Los Angeles by Major General George E. Armstrong, Army Surgeon General. He said that United States soldiers, wounded in Korea, who reach hospitals near the front had more than twice as good a chance of recovery as did soldiers wounded in the Second Word War. The medical corps, which has always been long on good hard work and short on publicity, warrants special commendation for this record. General Armstrong indicated that although body armor experiments had been favorable, teamwork between the medical corps, rescue troops, and helicopters had been an important factor in the diminishing death rate. (Namenwirth and Bibbee, 1975)

The essential point is that interpretations of statistical manipulations based on quantified text *must* be validated by reference to the text itself. Examination of exemplary texts, here identified by extreme factor scores, will provide direct evidence for or against particular interpretations. Similar themes in those editorials with similar extreme factor scores provide direct textual evidence that the same "story" is found repeatedly in a subset of texts, and consequently that the substantive conclusions are not artifacts of the content classification or statistical techniques employed. Also, examination of the texts may suggest the need to revise or discard the initial interpretation of the factor.

Note that interpretation is in part an art. Those who naively believe that data or texts speak for themselves (the doctrine of radical empiricism) are mistaken. The content analyst contributes factual and theoretical knowledge to the interpretation (see Namenwirth and Weber, 1987).

Interpretation cannot be the only goal of content analysis. As Krippendorff (1980) rightly stresses, the content of texts, however interpreted, must be related either to the context that produced them or to some consequent state of affairs. The following section shows that variation in the two sets of themes identified by Namenwirth and Bibbee (1975) is related to the type of newspaper in which they appeared.

TABLE 3.7

Prestige (Elite) Versus Mass Newspapers as a
Determinant of Selected Themes in Editorials

Factor 1: Control of the Social Environment		
	Mass Newspapers	*Prestige Newspapers*
Mean Factor Score:	1.56	−1.56
$F = 112.70$, df = 1,270, $p < .05$, ω^2 (%) = 77		

Factor 2: Control of the Physical Environment		
	Mass Newspapers	*Prestige Newspapers*
Mean Factor Score:	−.75	.75
$F = 20.24$, df = 1,270, $p < .05$, ω^2 (%) = 38		

SOURCE: Adapted from Namenwirth and Bibbee (1975)

Accounting for Content 1:
Characteristics of the Message Producers

As evidence of validity, many content analysis studies rely on internal consistency (i.e., showing that the textual evidence is more consistent with the interpretation). Even when explanations are offered, researchers seldom determine how strongly content-analytic variables are related to external factors. This section presents further results showing that variation in the themes documented above depends in part on characteristics of the message source (newspapers).

Namenwirth and Bibbee (1975) used an analysis of variance design[49] to assess the effect of newspaper type (elite or mass) on variation in themes, while simultaneously controlling for city (Boston, New York, or Washington) and time period during the Korean War.[50]

As Table 3.7 indicates, type of newspaper accounts for substantial variation in concern with control of the social environment and control of the physical environment: 77% and 38%, respectively. Mass newspapers stress parochial themes; prestige newspapers stress cosmopolitan ones. In addition, the mass press stresses military themes; the prestige press stresses economic problems. This result may not be surprising, because few sons of the elite classes were dying in Korea and because economic problems and controls directly affected the economic basis of the elite classes and their institutions.

The amount of variance in the dependent variables explained by type of newspaper is much larger than in most studies not using time-series analysis (econometricians routinely account for 90% or more of the variance in the dependent variable). Two other themes reported by Namenwirth and Bibbee, however, did less well: Type of newspaper accounted for only 15% and 6% of the variance, respectively. Also, not all of the variance of the first two themes was accounted for by type of newspaper. This means, first, that other causes of newspaper content were not included in the design and hence were not controlled. Second, some variance was accounted for by the two control variables, city and time. Third, error variance was not excluded from the factor scores,[51] and some unreliability remains.[52] This unreliability probably attenuates the relationship between themes and other variables.

Accounting for Content 2:
Changes in the Socioeconomic System

One of the most interesting and important applications of content analysis may be in cross-language designs. This section briefly describes findings from a small study undertaken to assess the cross-language validity of one content analysis dictionary.[53]

The development of valid and reliable content-analytic instruments for the analysis of German-language text is a prerequisite for comparing quantitatively the relationships between changes in symbol usage, economy, society, and polity in German and English-speaking countries. Consequently, the investigators carried out a small study to evaluate the cross-language validity and reliability of some content categories from the Lasswell Value Dictionary (Namenwirth and Weber, 1987: chapter 2; Zuell, Weber, and Mohler, 1989). Their immediate empirical question concerned the relationship between concern with wealth in the speeches of the German Kaiser 1871-1912 and economic fluctuations.

Specifically they hypothesized two theoretical concepts: *wealth concerns* and *economic performance*. Each of these unobserved or latent variables is measured by two or more observed variables. Three WEALTH categories of the Lasswell Value Dictionary measure wealth concerns: WEALTH-PARTICIPANTS, WEALTH-TRANSACTIONS, and WEALTH-OTHER. As noted in Chapter 2, the first category contains the names of those persons or positions involved in the creation, maintenance, and transfer of wealth, such as *banker*. The TRANSACTIONS category contains references to exchanges of wealth, such as *buying, selling,* and *borrowing*. The WEALTH-OTHER category contains wealth-related words not classified in the other two categories.

The measurement of economic performance in the period 1871-1912 is difficult because reasonably valid and reliable economic data from this period are usually lacking. The investigators were fortunate, however, to locate the prices of wheat and rye on the Berlin wholesale grain market between 1871 and 1912. Grain prices have two qualities important for the study: First, they are public information well-known to most people, either directly or indirectly through the price of bread and other grain products. Second, grain prices are less likely to be subject to measurement errors than are composite price indices or national accounts data based on aggregation across many units, such as estimates of gross national product. Although there may have been some regional variation in grain prices, the investigators believe that the data accurately represent the prices of these two widely used commodities.

What is the relationship between grain prices and economic performance? Prices are related positively to economic performance; that is, the price of grain and the economy tend to rise and fall together because price levels are in part an indicator of the inflation that often occurs in expanding economies. It is certainly true that other factors — such as weather, foreign trade, and the availability of substitutes — influence prices. Only that part of variation in wheat and rye prices that the two variables have in common, however, is used in the composite measure of economic performance. The remaining variance in wheat and rye prices is considered to be error variance consisting of measurement errors and variance because of factors other than economic performance.

If grain prices are an indicator of economic performance, then what is the relationship between economic performance and wealth concerns? Previous analyses of American and British political documents and economic change (Namenwirth, 1969b; Namenwirth and Weber, 1987) show that economic performance and wealth concerns are related inversely: As the economy improves there is less concern with wealth, whereas a declining economy is associated with increasing wealth concerns. In short, higher levels of concern with economic matters are associated with economic adversity. Thus the investigators were pleased to find that the data showed a negative relationship between economic performance and wealth concerns in the Kaiser's speeches from 1871 to 1912 — that is, changes in the rate of change of the economy (acceleration) were negatively related to wealth concerns.[54]

Figure 3.3 shows the structure of the causal model and the parameters to be estimated from the data. These unknown parameters (coefficients) are estimated using the LISREL approach to the analysis of covariance structures (Jöreskog and Sörbom, 1979, 1984). The general LISREL model consists of two parts: the measurement model and the structural equation model. The measurement model defines how the latent or unobserved variables are related to observed variables. The structural equation model specifies the structure of causal relationships among latent variables and among the error variances. In the model proposed above, the observed variables are content categories, and the latent variables are economic performance and wealth concerns.

Besides estimating the measurement and structural equation models simultaneously, the LISREL model also estimates how well the predicted covariance matrix reproduces or fits the observed covariance (or correlation) matrix. This indicator is an approximation to chi square with appropriate degrees of freedom for the number of free and constrained parameters. The lower the chi square, the better the fit of the model to the data.

Table 3.8 and Figure 3.3 present the results.[55] Some caution is necessary in the interpretation of these results, because the LISREL goodness-of-fit statistics assume large sample sizes. The chi square for the overall fit of the model is not significant (.905 with 4 df, $p < .9238$), which suggests that there is a very small probability of finding a better fitting model. Almost all the estimated parameters are twice their standard errors. The t statistic for the causal coefficient between economic performance and wealth concerns is just under 2, at 1.98. Also, the t statistic for the error variance of the dependent variable (wealth concerns) is .667, which in this case suggests that there is very little error variance left (i.e., the residual or error variance is not different from zero). This is not surprising because economic performance accounts for 73% of the variance in wealth concerns. The coefficient indicating the loading of WEALTH-PARTICIPANTS on wealth concerns (LY3) is not significant, but given the overall results of the model and the low number of cases, the researchers decided to leave this variable in the model.

Finally, the magnitude and direction of the relationship between wealth concerns and economic performance show that the WEALTH categories the investigators constructed for German text are quite reli-

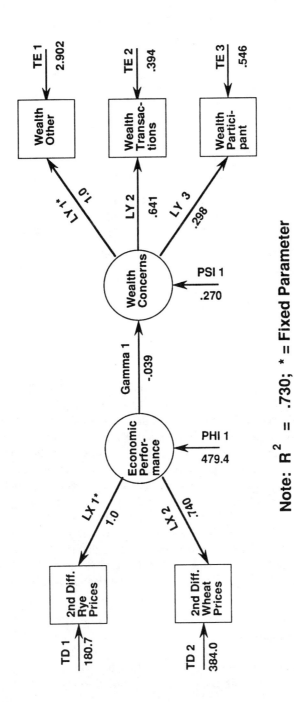

Note: R² = .730; * = Fixed Parameter

Figure 3.3. Structural Model Relating Economic Performance and Wealth Concerns in Kaiser Speeches, 1871-1912

SOURCE: Adapted from Weber (1984a)

TABLE 3.8

LISREL Parameter Estimates: Economic Performance and
Wealth Concerns in Kaiser Speeches, 1871-1912*

Parameter	Unstd. Coef.	Std. Err.	t
LX1**	1.000		
LX2	.740	.275	2.690
TDI	180.700	155.100	1.165
TD2	384.000	128.000	3.000
PHI1	479.400	220.800	2.171
GAMMA1	−.039	.020	1.980
PSI1	.270	.404	.667
LY1**	1.000		
LY2	.641	.296	2.166
LY3	.298	.195	1.528
TE1	2.902	.859	3.378
TE2	.394	.184	2.143
TE3	.546	.150	3.646

LISREL Estimates, N = 31

*See Figure 3.3 for structure of model.
** Parameter fixed to 1 for purposes of identification.
SOURCE: Adapted from Weber (1984a)

able and valid. As predicted, this relationship is negative. The size of
the coefficient (−.039) suggests that a 10-mark change in the rate of
change of prices caused an increase (or decrease) of 4 wealth words per
1000. Because of the content-analytic procedures employed, it is likely
that the size of the unstandardized coefficient understates the relationship between wealth-related issues and economic performance. The
investigators counted only those words that by themselves indicate
wealth concerns rather than total words in sentences dealing with
economic problems. Had the latter been done, the size of the coefficient
might be substantially higher because the variance of the dependent
variable would be higher. It is also worth noting that if all the observed
and latent variables had zero means and standard deviations of 1.0, then
the coefficient between economic performance and wealth concerns
would be −.855, which is certainly a substantial relationship.[56]

Concluding Remarks

The techniques presented in this chapter illustrate several possibilities for content analysis ranging from detailed analysis of word or

phrase usage (KWIC lists and concordances) to multivariate analysis based on quantification. Other quantitative means of analysis were omitted because of space limitations. These include regression analysis, time-series regression models, discriminant analysis, and cluster analysis.

The spirit of the preceding presentation is illustrative and didactic. It is worth repeating that there is no single right way to do content analysis. Instead, investigators must judge what methods are appropriate for their substantive problems. Given the ubiquity of computers, there is a real danger that as software for content analysis becomes distributed more widely, as the costs of encoding texts in machine-readable form continue to decline, and as the opportunity for capturing texts directly from other electronic media increases (e.g., newspaper editing and composing systems, word processors and typesetters, and newswires), the danger of mindless content analysis will also increase. One reason content analysis is not used more widely is that it is difficult and time-consuming to do well. Computers eliminate some of the drudgery, but time, effort, skill, and art are required to produce results, interpretations, and explanations that are valid and theoretically interesting.

Suggestions for Further Reading

Anyone thinking of doing content analysis would be well advised to look carefully at Stone et al. (1966). Namenwirth and Weber (1987) apply updated versions of these techniques to political documents, newspaper editorials, and speeches. Related methodological concerns are addressed in Kelly and Stone (1975) and Zuell et al. (1989). Rosengren (1981) presents several studies of the Swedish symbol system using human-coded content analysis. The early classics of Berelson (1952), Lasswell (e.g., Lasswell, Leites, et al., 1965; Lasswell, Lerner, and Pool, 1952), and Pool (1951, 1952a, 1952b, 1959) are still worthwhile reading to see what kind of problems they addressed and how they resolved them.

There is also a large "computers and the humanities" literature, including a journal by that title currently published by the Paradigm Press. Papers from several conferences on computers and the humanities also have been published, including Ager, Knowles, and Smith (1979); Aitken, Bailey, and Hamilton-Smith (1973); Jones and Church-house (1976); and Wisbey (1971). A related text is Oakman (1980).

Salton (1989) discusses text processing from a computer-science perspective focusing on information retrieval. There is a huge and still-growing literature on natural language processing and computational linguistics. Allen (1987) provides an excellent introduction to modern methods for computer processing of language. Winograd and Flores (1986) provide an important philosophical and social critique of such endeavors.

4. ISSUES IN CONTENT ANALYSIS

Content analysis procedures create quantitative indicators that assess the degree of attention or concern devoted to cultural units such as themes, categories, or issues. The investigator then interprets and explains the results using relevant theories. This chapter considers four key aspects of the content analysis process:

- *measurement* — the assignment of numbers that stand for some aspect of the text
- *indication* — the inference by the investigator of some unmeasured quality or characteristic of the text from those numbers
- *representation* — techniques for describing syntactic, semantic, or pragmatic aspects of texts
- *interpretation* — the translation of the meaning in text into some other abstract analytical or theoretical language

For each of these processes, difficulties exist that may detract from the reliability of the procedures or from the validity of substantive conclusions based on them. This chapter discusses some of these problems in order to help researchers make more informed choices about their procedures, to help in understanding the limitations of currently available content analysis procedures, and to suggest new lines of research that may (at least in part) resolve these problems.

Measurement

In content analysis, measurement consists of counting the occurrences of meaning units such as specific words, phrases, content categories, and themes. Regardless of whether the text is coded by humans or by computers, two standard measurement practices are using the percentage (or proportion) transformation to control for document length[57] and counting each occurrence of a word or other meaning unit equally. Each of these practices leads to serious difficulties that require attention.

The Percentage Transformation. This section addresses four specific problems that arise from using the percentage transformation to control for document length. First, the percentage or proportion has limited range and is asymptotic; consequently, the resulting measurement is not linear (for example, an increase from 5% to 10% is not the same as an increase from 60% to 65%).

Second, statisticians have shown that the mean and variance of percentages are not independent. Therefore, when used as the dependent variable in analysis of variance designs, proportions are subjected to an arcsin square root transformation, a procedure recommended by statisticians to make the mean and variance independent (see, e.g., Freeman and Tukey, 1950; Schuessler, 1971: 411-416). Additional research is required to determine if percentages based on textual data — with or without transformation — create problems in statistical estimation and inference when used with multivariate procedures other than ANOVA, such as factor analysis or the LISREL approach to structural equation models.

Third, different measurement strategies may imply different theoretical assumptions. For example, the percentage distribution may be inconsistent with the hypothesis that concern with secular rather than sacred themes increases linearly over time. Extended far enough into the future, such a trend must eventually exceed 100%. Investigators therefore should consider whether their measurement procedures unwittingly conflict with their epistemological and methodological assumptions and substantive theories.

Fourth, many of the statistical procedures used by content analysts make distributional assumptions that probably are violated by the percentage distribution. For example, content analysis data are unlikely to be either univariate or multivariate normal.

Rather than using percentages or proportions, some colleagues (in personal communications) have suggested instead modeling frequency counts generated by content analysis as a Poisson process and then using statistical estimation procedures based on this distribution. Most content-analytic studies thus far have relied on the robustness of factor analysis, curve-fitting, ANOVA, and other statistical procedures combined with validation techniques based on examination of the original text. Still, additional research is needed to assess whether the robustness of these statistical methods really compensates for the deviations of most content analysis data from the Gaussian normal distribution.

Counting Occurrences Equally. The standard practice of counting equally each occurrence of a given semantic unit engenders two different problems. The first is that each of the words classified in a given category may not reflect that category to the same extent. The second is that subsequent mentions of a category or topic may require greater effort than the first few mentions.

To explain: The measurement procedures of content analysis are based on frequency counts of semantically equivalent textual units such as words, word senses, phrases, issues, or themes. The semantic equivalence that underlies the procedures described earlier in this volume is *connotative categorical equivalence.*[58] Textual units are connotative categorically equivalent if they signify or suggest certain meanings, ideas, and so forth in addition to their explicit or primary meanings. For example, in one category scheme, both *bonus* and *allowance* are classified in the category WEALTH because they share a common connotation — namely, economic matters.

Each word classified in a particular category need not equally represent the category content. Nevertheless, counting each entry equally is desirable because we currently lack procedures that reliably and validly assign weights indicating the unequal representation of category content by different entries in a single category (see Namenwirth and Weber, 1987: chapter 8). Neither can we now handle situations where the degree of representation may vary across sets of documents or over time.[59]

A different problem arises when investigators count equally each occurrence of each entry in the same category in a given document. For example, the 25th occurrence of an entry in the category AFFECTION is given the same weight or importance as the 5th occurrence or as the 125th. Equal counting is a practical simplification that content analysts believe works well in most circumstances, but reality is probably much more complicated.

Specifically, content analysts long have assumed that the more a text contains mentions of a particular category, the more it is concerned with it. Philip J. Stone (personal communication) has conjectured that the initial mention of a word (or category, theme, or topic) required more effort or energy than successive mentions. Put another way, raising a new topic requires more energy or effort than continuing the previous one (topic avoidance is addressed later). If raising the topic at all requires an effort, what about continuing the topic through succeeding mentions? There exists a point after which each succeeding mention requires more rather than less effort. This is so because:

- Stylistic considerations may cause authors to substitute pronouns where possible.[60]
- Continuing concern with a particular category (e.g., WEALTH) may lead to redundancy or repetition so that the amount of information being communicated declines as the text continues.
- If there are contextual constraints on text length — for example, the amount of time available for a State of the Union address — continued attention to one issue, theme, or category, precludes attention to other topics.
- Even if there are not contextual constraints, the resources available for text production are surely finite. Text producers therefore typically will allocate their efforts to a range of issues and themes.

Not all topics are equally difficult to raise. In contemporary America, for example, it may well be easier for political parties to address economic issues such as trade and deficits than the history and current plight of Native Americans living precariously on reservations. Thus some topics may require much more effort to raise than others. For reasons noted above, however, continued attention to a topic requires still greater effort. Therefore, equal counting of each instance does not reflect changes in the level of effort required to maintain the topic.

Also, the assertion that zero mention requires no effort is plainly wrong at times. Keeping issues from being mentioned may also require much effort. The Freudian notions that unconscious ego urges drive us and that we must repress ourselves and others to maintain civilization are relevant here. Under circumstances that have yet to be explored systematically, the lack of mention therefore can be of great significance.

These ideas suggest that further research should examine the consequences of equal counting on validity and reliability in general, and on measurement in particular.

Indication

As noted earlier, the term *indication* refers to inferences made by the investigator of some unmeasured or latent characteristics of text using numbers that represent some manifest aspect of the text. For example, as shown in the previous chapter, factor analysis often is used to infer themes in text. More subtle examples are presented shortly. Some critics believe that indication is problematic because they question the reliability and validity of all inferences concerning latent characteristics of text, or of such inferences in the absence of accompanying detailed syntactic and semantic information.

This section addresses two important aspects of indication. The first concerns the rationale for analyzing latent characteristics of the text at all. The second concerns latent characteristics of texts that may not be discernible through detailed semantic analysis without quantification.

In social science research we often use statistical procedures (such as factor analysis, structural equation models, and simple correlations) that suggest or assume the existence of unmeasured or latent variables. As most often applied in content analysis, the unit of analysis in these statistical procedures is the entire document.[61] Therefore, latent variables indicate features of each entire text (or other coding or analytic unit, such as paragraphs, chapters, or document sections). These latent-variable models raise interesting problems and possibilities not often met in social research (Mohler, personal communication). In latent-indicator models of mental ideas such as attitudes, for example, the investigator can never observe directly mental states that validate the interpretation of the results (and given the problematic relationships between attitudes and behavior, it is not possible to infer the former from the latter, either). A different situation, however, exists in content analysis. Here the investigator *can* examine the relationship between latent variables and the original text being analyzed.

If one has observables such as text, why bother with quantification and latent-indicator models at all? There are several reasons. First, counting generates results that allow for more precise comparisons among texts. Second, we want to know how much more (or less) attention is devoted to some issues than to others. Third, quantitative analytical procedures often reveal similarities and differences among texts that would be difficult, if not impossible, to detect otherwise.

Investigators often find that covariation among observed variables suggests substantively interesting features of texts that otherwise would not be apparent. The fact that latent variables so inferred actually are derived from observable texts makes them no less useful. Rather, examining the observable text is an important opportunity to improve the interpretation and validation of the substantive findings.

As noted in the introductory chapter, the coding and quantitative techniques discussed in this volume often are criticized because they do not make much use of the syntactical and semantic information in each sentence. Nevertheless, these quantitative methods often permit inferences that probably could not be made by other means.

For example, several studies (Namenwirth and Weber, 1987: chapter 9) have found similar positive correlations between four pairs of categories: (1) IF and SURE (or UNDERSTATE[62] and OVERSTATE), (2) POSITIVE AFFECT and NEGATIVE AFFECT, (3) POWER CONFLICT and POWER COOPERATION, and (4) POWER AUTHORITATIVE and POWER AUTHORITATIVE PARTICIPANTS. What do these correlations tell us?

- If a document uses many UNDERSTATE words, such as *ambiguous, apparent,* and *little,* it is also likely to use many OVERSTATE words, such as *absolute, natural,* and *necessary.* But this finding leaves open whether these classes of words do or do not occur in the same sentence or paragraph context. Furthermore, Namenwirth and Weber (1987: chapter 9) interpret this correlational finding itself as *indicating* that those documents high in OVERSTATE and UNDERSTATE words discuss matters very defensively compared with those documents with few words in these categories. But this is not to say that such documents explicitly state that they are defensive about whatever they discuss. In fact, they rarely do.

- Similarly, the positive correlation between POSITIVE AFFECT (*attachment, beneficial,* and *inspire*) and NEGATIVE AFFECT (*adverse, neglect,* and *obnoxious*) first suggests that documents are most often either affect-laden or affect-neutral, and, second, indirectly tells whether and to what extent particular documents are of one kind or another. Documents rarely will state this fact outright. Instead, these correlations suggest something about the mood, tone, or style of documents.

- Third, several studies have found a positive correlation between POWER CONFLICT (*agitate, encroachments,* and *rebellion*) and POWER COOPERATION (*solidarity, supporter,* and *unanimous*). Thus documents with a high frequency of one will displace a high frequency of the other.

- We also find that POWER COOPERATION and POWER CONFLICT are usually correlated negatively with another pair of categories, namely, POWER AUTHORITATIVE (*administer, reign, statute*) and POWER AUTHORITATIVE PARTICIPANT (*administrator, regiment, tribunal*). The latter positively correlated cluster indicates a concern with consensual power that is a facility of the entire society (Lehman, 1977; Namenwirth and Weber, 1987: 149). These findings show that documents are preoccupied with either consensual or conflictual power concerns, but not both at the same time. More important, whatever their power concerns, documents rarely state them explicitly: they "merely" are indicated.

Thus our commonsense impressions about the utility of semantic information in narrow contexts reflect a limited (but still important) truth, as these examples also show. In fact, content-analytic procedures that restrict themselves to themes that are stated explicitly would certainly miss many of these important indications.

Representation

The kind of text classification and content analysis described in this volume is criticized sometimes for not utilizing essential syntactic or semantic features of language or text in the analysis. These critics often call attention to the fact that both human-based coding procedures and the computer systems described here do not encode or represent the richness of language or of specific texts. One way that the meaning of words, phrases, or other textual units is represented is through classification into a set of categories. In assigning meaning units to categories, not all connotations or nuances of meaning are pertinent. It does not make much sense to insist on linguistic distinctions that are more fine-grained than the distinctions made by the category scheme. Thus content classification procedures safely ignore irrelevant distinctions. But what is a relevant distinction?

In the early and mid-1970s, Stone and his collaborators (Kelly and Stone, 1975; Zuell, Weber, and Mohler, 1989) developed an improved version of the General Inquirer computer system for content analysis that can differentiate among the various senses of homographs. For example, is the word *frame* a noun or a verb? Does *kind* refer to a class of objects or a benevolent disposition? Consider the word *state*. The General Inquirer distinguishes six different senses or uses:

- state (noun; body politic or area of government)
- situation (e.g., *state of science*)
- "to state" (verb; to declare)
- "state of affairs" (idiom; situation)
- "united states" (idiom; handled by *United*)
- "ship of state" (idiom; government, handled by *ship*)

Kelly and Stone's (1975) disambiguation of *state* is itself a simplification.[63] The *Random House Dictionary of the English Language* (college edition) lists 17 different senses for *state*. The *Oxford English Dictionary* lists at least 41 different meanings. Not every shade of meaning or nuance, however, will be relevant to a particular investigation. Thus in the interest of parsimony, perhaps only 5 or 10 usages of *state* may be sufficient.

In short, although more powerful text analysis systems will be useful, some distinctions may not be worth maintaining. Convenience and parsimony are important factors in deciding how much detail to maintain.

Interpretation

Interpretation consists of translating one set of linguistic or linguistically expressed elements into another (Namenwirth and Weber, 1987: chapters 2 and 8). This translation or "mapping" procedure leads to several difficulties that are explored best through an example.

Weber analyzed British Speeches from the Throne 1689-1972 (Namenwirth and Weber, 1987: chapters 4 and 5; Weber, 1981, 1982). For each of the documents, the content analysis procedures created quantitative measures of attention devoted to various content categories. Subsequent analysis of these quantitative data suggested the existence of political issues or themes that recurred periodically in these texts. For example, Weber (Namenwirth and Weber, 1987: chapter 4) identified four issues or themes that recurred approximately every 72 years[64] during the period 1689-1795. Consider the following excerpt from the speech of 1690 (Namenwirth and Weber, 1987):

> It is sufficiently known how earnestly I have endeavored to extinguish, or at least compose, all differences amongst my subjects, and to that end, how often have I recommended an Act of Indemnity to the last Parliament; but since that part of it which related to the preventing of private suits, is already enacted, and because debates of that nature must take up more of your time than can now be spared from the dispatch of those other things which are absolutely necessary for our common safety, I intend to send you an Act of Grace, with exceptions of some few persons only, but such as may be sufficient to show my great dislike of their crimes; and, at the same time, my readiness to extend protection to all my other subjects, who

will thereby see that they can recommend themselves to me by no other methods, than what the law prescribes, which shall always be the only rules of my government.

Now compare the preceding with excerpt with the following one given in 1757:

I have had such ample experience of the loyalty and good affections of my faithful subjects towards me, my family, and government, in all circumstances, that I am confident they are not to be shaken. But I cannot avoid taking notice of that spirit of disorder, which has shown itself amongst the common people, in some parts of the Kingdom. Let me recommend it to you, to do your part in discouraging and suppressing such abuses and for maintaining the law, and lawful authority. If anything shall be found wanting, to explain or enforce what may have been misunderstood or misrepresented, I am persuaded it will not escape your attention. Nothing can be so conducive to the defense of all that is dear to us, as well as for reducing our enemies to reason, as union and harmony amongst ourselves.

Many readers will agree that these excerpts address the same underlying issue or theme, but might disagree over what to name it. Let us briefly postpone naming the common theme until after we consider interpretation itself.

The process of interpretation constitutes translation from one language to another (Namenwirth and Weber, 1987). Each language consists of a set of rules that define what constitutes a valid sentence in the language. Using these rules, speakers of the language can generate a virtually infinite number of sentences. Considering a text in one language, translation consists in large part of mapping the syntactic and semantic structures that comprise the text in the first language into structures that are valid for the second and that convey the meaning of the first.

As is well-known, translation can be a difficult process (Steiner, 1975). A procedure, however, for checking the validity of a translation exists — namely, back-translation. Here the text in the target language is translated back into the original and then compared with the original. When the back-translation and the original text are the same, then the first translation is valid. Note that this kind of translation is bidirectional or reversible: Once investigators have translated the text into the second language they usually can reconstruct the original text. Note also that there may be only one or very few translations that are valid. Not all translations, however, are reversible.

The primary concern here is with irreversible or unidirectional transformations that map the content of texts into more abstract, usually theoretical structures. For content analysis, this specialized language is usually the social science theory (or theories) used by the investigator to interpret the text and explain the substantive results. Here the mapping is from the many words of the text into fewer and more abstract categories and into relations suggested by the theory.

Note that in the excerpts above, the words — let alone the syntax — used to convey the basic themes are hardly identical. For example, the first excerpt begins by discussing differences among subjects of the King, whereas the second excerpt begins by discussing the loyalty and good affections of the subjects. Some differences reflect differing historical circumstances. Coming two years after the Glorious Revolution of 1688, the first excerpt discusses an Act of Indemnity and Act of Grace. Given during the Seven Years' War, the second excerpt ends with a reference to foreign enemies and internal cohesion.

These differences aside, sociologists and political scientists usually would choose one of two principal theoretical and conceptual frameworks for labeling the common underlying issue. Marxists and other conflict theorists might say that these excerpts deal with conflict between the common people on the one side and the aristocracy, commercial interests, and the incipient capitalist classes on the other.[65] Weber (Namenwirth and Weber, 1987: chapter 4) chose to interpret the common underlying issue as reflecting what Bales and Parsons refer to as *integrative* concerns, whose principle focus is the coordination of the various subgroups in society (or other social system).[66]

As this example illustrates, there is no one-to-one mapping between text and theory. Also, the translation from text to theory is not reversible. One could generate virtually an infinite number of excerpts whose interpretation is as an instance of integrative themes in the Bales/Parsons sense. Thus the strategy of back-translation is not available to us as a means of validating the mapping from text to theory.

Given that differing, perhaps antithetical theoretical frameworks can be used to interpret these texts, what should we conclude? First, a variety of interpretations usually will be available and the investigator must choose. It is inappropriate to pursue a fruitless quest in search of the "true" or the "valid" interpretation. As Slater (1966) points out, it is not the validity of an interpretation per se that is at issue, but rather the salience of an interpretation given one or another theory. Second, just as it is true that quantitative data do not speak for themselves (i.e., that the doctrine of radical empiricism is false), so is it true that texts do not speak for themselves either. The investigator must do the speaking and the language of that speech is the language of theory.

Concluding Remarks

This chapter addressed several problems that arise when text is analyzed for social science purposes. These difficulties are inherent in the fundamental processes of content analysis — namely, measurement, indication, representation, and interpretation. Not only are they fundamental to content analysis, these processes are fundamental to most inquiry in the humanities and sciences. Interpretation and representation, for example, entail difficulties that are neither understood widely nor resolved easily. A much more sustained, interdisciplinary effort is required.

Suggestions for Further Reading

The techniques discussed in this volume were developed before recent advances in other disciplines concerning language and understanding. The literature has grown huge, but some of the literature not mentioned here previously includes Boden (1987, 1988), Brady and Berwick (1983), Dyer (1983), Weizenbaum (1976), and Winograd (1983).

APPENDIX
Computer Software and Text Data Archives

TEXTPACK, a comprehensive software system for text analysis, is now being distributed for a nominal charge by the Computer Department/ ZUMA/ The Center for Surveys, Methods, and Analysis/ B2,1/ D-6800 Mannheim 1/ Federal Republic of Germany. This software will run on microcomputers, workstations, minicomputers, and mainframes provided they have a FORTRAN compiler that supports the 1977 standard. A version for MS-DOS personal computers is now available from ZUMA. TEXTPACK documentation is available in either English or German.

As desired by the investigator, TEXTPACK V will perform or generate frequency counts of words, key-word-in-context (KWIC) lists, key-word-out-of-context (KWOC) lists, comparisons of vocabularies, cross-references, procedures for iterative dictionary construction, retrievals of text units, reduction of text via go-stop lists, and tagging (OR function for all systems: OR, AND, NOT, BEFORE, AFTER, NOT functions for IBM and Siemens versions). In addition, there are interfaces for the major statistical packages. Full disambiguation, however, is not available at this time.

The General Inquirer III system for classifying and analyzing text by computer is now available from ZUMA at the address above. This software classifies the many words of texts into content categories by looking up each word in a content analysis dictionary. The dictionary contains a list of words — a vocabulary — and for each word the category or categories in which it is to be classified.

The General Inquirer is written in the PL/1 language for IBM MVS and VM operating systems. Although the PL/1 source code is distributed, the system should not be considered portable to other (and especially non-IBM) computing environments. The General Inquirer was created many years ago when batch computer systems prevailed. Thus the system is not particularly user-friendly. The full documentation for the system and related material is now available as a ZUMA publication (Zuell, Weber, and Mohler, 1989). Together with the General Inquirer software, ZUMA is distributing three large and well-established dictionaries, namely, the Lasswell Value Dictionary and two versions (IV-3 and IV-4) of the Harvard Psychosociological Dictionary. These are documented in Zuell et al. (1989). The General Inquirer runs on all IBM mainframes using MVS or VM operating systems; a PL/1 compiler must be available because the system is delivered as program source code and must therefore be compiled; the system SORT utility is required by some General Inquirer routines.

The current version of the Oxford Concordance Program for mainframes is version 2. This is distributed by Oxford University Computing Service. Please address inquiries to OCP, Oxford University Computing Service, 13 Banbury Road, Oxford OX2 6NN, England, e-mail OCP@VAX.OX.AC.UK. Micro-OCP is a version of OCP for the IBM PC and compatibles. It requires at least 512K, a hard disk, and DOS 3.0

or higher. It is completely compatible with mainframe OCP V2 (i.e., files can be transferred from the PC to mainframe and run without change). Micro-OCP is published by Oxford Electronic Publishing, Oxford University Press, Walton Street, Oxford OX2 6DP, England. The program is documented in Susan Hockey and Jeremy Martin's *OCP Users' Manual Version 2,* Oxford University Computing Service; *Micro-OCP Manual,* obtainable from Oxford University Press, address above — this is not sold in bookstores, only by mail order from OUP; and Hockey and Martin (1987).

Software for text analysis often is described in the journal *Computers and the Humanities,* currently published by Paradigm Press, P. O. Box 1057, Osprey, FL 33559-1057.

At this writing, few text data sets have been archived and made publicly accessible. The ICPSR at the University of Michigan has at least two text data sets created by Holsti and North. One contains a sample of the replies to the British Speeches from the Throne given at the opening of each session of Parliament. Another file contains the speeches of the German Kaiser. The latter data set was found to be incomplete and contains numerous errors. The former data set is documented poorly.

The entire texts of Democratic and Republican (Whig) Party platforms 1844-1964 have been archived at the Roper Center, University of Connecticut, Storrs, CT 06268. They are available on computer tape through the Roper Center for a small fee. These data are also available in Europe from the Zentralarchiv für Empirische Sozialforschung/Bachmer Strasse 40/D-5000 Köln 31/FRG. In addition, British Speeches from the Throne at the opening of Parliament 1689-1972 have been archived at the same institutions.

NOTES

1. Various authors have proposed format definitions of content analysis. For example, Stone et al. (1966: 5) state: "Content analysis is any research technique for making inferences by systematically and objectively identifying specified characteristics within text." Krippendorff (1980: 21) defines the method as follows: "Content analysis is a research technique for making replicative and valid inferences from data to their context." Krippendorff is right to emphasize the relationship between the content of texts and their institutional, societal, or cultural contexts. See Chapter 3 and Namenwirth and Weber (1987) for extended discussions.

2. Other perspectives on text analysis include linguistics, psychology, and artificial intelligence. As noted in Chapter 3, there is also a large "computers and the humanities" literature that partly overlaps the concerns of this volume.

3. *Meaning* refers to shared as opposed to private understandings.

4. Category names are shown in small capital letters.

5. Another, more qualitative or clinical tradition of content analysis is not emphasized here. See, for example, George (1959a, 1959b), Berelson (1952: chapter 3), and some of the articles in a special issue of Qualitative Sociology, 1984 (volume 7, numbers 1 and 2).

6. Various systems for computer-aided content analysis are more or less successful in distinguishing among various word meanings and connotations. This problem and several resolutions are discussed later.

7. *Construct validity* has been used to refer to two different types of validity; hence there is some confusion over the term. Cook and Campbell (1979: 59) use the term to refer to "the possibility that the operations which are meant to represent a particular cause or effect construct can be construed in terms or more than one construct." Others, following Cronbach and Meehl (1955) use the term *construct validity* to refer to the fit between data and constructs suggested by theory. The present discussion uses the former definition, and following Brinberg and McGrath (1982), refers to the latter definition as *hypothesis validity*, which is discussed below.

8. This is what Janis (1965) refers to as *indirect* validation, which he suggests is the main form of validation for content analysis. Hypothesis validity, however, has an important weakness: If the relationship between a content and a noncontent variable is counter to theory, does this invalidate the variables or the hypothesis?

9. There is nothing inherent in content-analysis techniques to limit predictive validity; rather, investigators seldom include assessments of predictive validity in their research designs.

10. This form of coding is based on Osgood, Suci, and Tannenbaum's (1957) evaluation assertion analysis (also see Holsti, 1966, 1969). A more sophisticated form is used by Axelrod (1976) and his collaborators in the coding of cognitive maps of political elites. Appendix One in that volume gives detailed coding rules.

11. Holsti (1969: 104-116) gives numerous examples of broad and narrow category schemes for content analysis.

12. It is routine to classify 90 to 95% of the words in most nonspecialized texts using general dictionaries. Also, they can be modified easily to handle highly specialized texts, such as the speeches of the presidents of American scientific associations (Namenwirth and Weber, 1987: chapter 7).

13. One reason content analysis did not blossom the way survey research did was that the lack of standardized procedures and measuring instruments worked against the accumulation of comparable results. See Namenwirth and Weber (1987: 195-196) for further discussion.

14. Many of the examples presented here use the General Inquirer system. At present, the TEXTPACK program mentioned in the Appendix will do everything that the General Inquirer can do, except disambiguation.

15. Table 2.1 is adapted from Namenwirth and Weber (1987) and Zuell et al. (1989). Table 2.2 is adapted from Dunphy et al. (1989).

16. Current computer software can distinguish the various senses of words with more than one meaning. This is discussed later.

17. For example, low-variance or oddly shaped distributions often cause problems in statistical estimation.

18. These distinctions are often semantic, but may also be syntactic — for example, identifying syntactic categories such as verbs, nouns, and modifiers. More precise classification results from correctly classifying modifiers, for example, into more specific classes such as adjectives and adverbs.

19. TEXTPACK V also has some capabilities for dealing with idioms.

20. Natural language-processing techniques developed in artificial intelligence and computer science are likely to provide a proper solution to the problem, but the software and hardware required will not be widely available for some time.

21. For simplicity, this and the next table omit the syntactic and marker categories assigned to each word. The latter are used in the disambiguation rules, and are not used normally in substantive interpretations.

22. Except for subcategory/category-total assignments (e.g., WEALTH-OTHER/WEALTH-TOTAL), the LVD is a single-classification dictionary. Words or word senses are assigned only to one substantive category. The Harvard IV-3 and Harvard IV-4 are multiple-classification dictionaries in which word senses may be assigned to more than one substantive category.

23. Intensity might be taken into account by multivariate models such as factor analysis and multidimensional scale. In that case intensity is indicated by magnitude of the factor loadings or MDS weights. See Namenwirth and Weber (1987: chapter 8) for a more technical discussion.

24. Note "Weber's Paradox" (Namenwirth and Weber, 1987: 36, 208n; Weber, 1983): Results using the Lasswell dictionary have not been interpreted or explained using Lasswell's theory, and results using the Harvard dictionary have not been interpreted or explained using Freudian or Parsonian theory. At present, general dictionaries should be considered useful, commonsense category schemes rather than the operationalization of a formal theory.

25. Krippendorff (1980: 157) distinguishes between "emic or indigenous rather than etic or imposed" categories, asserting without evidence that only the former are semantically valid. This raises sticky problems concerning both category schemes and manifest versus latent content. See Namenwirth and Weber (1987) for an extended discussion.

26. Factor analyzing word counts to infer themes has a long history, which is reviewed by Iker (1974). Stefflre (1965) is an early programmatic statement. Moreover, each approach entails a different measurement model. Specifically, first-order exploratory factor analysis is the statistical model that corresponds to inferring themes from word covariation. The measurement model for single-classification-assumed dictionaries corresponds to a restricted second-order confirmatory factor analysis (Namenwirth and Weber, 1987: chapter 8). I am unaware of any attempt to analyze the same texts using both measurement models. Therefore, it is uncertain whether these different approaches yield similar or different substantive findings.

27. Both the Harvard and Lasswell dictionaries emphasize institutional aspects of social life. In addition, Zvi Namenwirth played a large role in the creation of the Lasswell and early Harvard dictionaries. Therefore, it is not surprising that his results did replicate across dictionaries.

28. Usually percentages or proportions are used to standardize for the length of the document or other unit of text. These create other problems for analysis, however, that are addressed in Chapter 4.

29. Several useful indicators of content are not discussed here. For example, one might assume that words, topics, or themes mentioned near the beginning of the text are more important than those mentioned near the end of the text. Also, as Holsti (1969) shows, one can code text for positive or negative (favorable or unfavorable) assertions. These examples were suggested by an anonymous reviewer.

30. In choosing a simple random sample, each member of the universe or population to be sampled has an equal probability of being included in the sample.

31. In choosing a stratified random sample, each member of each subclass of the population has an equal probability of being included in the sample, but a different proportion of each subclass may be chosen. Put another way, the probability of a particular member of the population being chosen depends on which subclass that member belongs to.

32. Where the meaning of a word changes over time, KWIC lists often reflect these changes. Usually this poses no problem, because new meanings frequently entail additional usages such as the change from verb to noun, noun to adjective, and so forth. As shown later, computers can distinguish the various senses of homographs. Consequently, changes in meaning can be taken into account.

33. This version of KWIC prints the keyword with all or most of the sentence in which it appears. In principle, however, there is no limit other than utility of the size of the context provided.

34. Depending on the goals of the content analysis, other senses could be distinguished (see Chapter 4).

35. The utility of ordered word-frequency lists was suggested by Ronald D. Brunner (personal communication). The number of words included in the table was determined by space limitations rather than substantive or methodological considerations.

36. In studies of disputed authorship, however, these types of words have been found to distinguish accurately between authors (e.g., Mosteller and Wallace, 1964).

37. A second assumption is that differences in word frequencies reflect differences in the attention of the message source. This is likely to be true for rank orders but not for absolute frequencies, because absolute frequencies are partly a function of document length.

38. In the computers and humanities literature these are called *collocations* (e.g., Berry-Rogghe, 1973; Firth, 1957; Geffroy, Lafon, Seidel, and Tournier, 1973; Haskel, 1971).

39. Very long sentences were broken up; plus signs represent semicolons.

40. This and the following section draw on a larger text data base consisting of Democratic and Republican party platforms 1844-1980 (Johnson, 1979, 1982) developed in collaboration with J. Zvi Namenwirth. See the Appendix for information regarding archived text data.

41. For each party, the data were standardized to a mean of zero and a standard deviation of 1.0 to eliminate differences of scale in the figure.

42. These results replicate and extend some of Namenwirth's (1969b) findings for the period 1844-1964.

43. Iker (1965, 1974; Iker and Harway, 1969), for example, factor-analyzed word-frequency counts. Another approach (Namenwirth, 1969a, 1970; Namenwirth and Bibbee, 1975; Namenwirth and Weber, 1987) applies factor analysis to category counts to identify themes in texts. The relative merits of these approaches have been discussed extensively elsewhere (Namenwirth and Weber, 1987: chapter 8; Weber, 1983).

44. This is a modification of the Harvard III Psychosocial dictionary documented in Stone et al. (1966: 169ff).

45. Some categories were eliminated because of low variance or because they did not discriminate between mass and elite papers.

46. The principal-components method is often confused with true factor analysis. The former excludes unique variances, but retains common and error variances. True factor analysis excludes both unique and error variances. Most, if not all factor analysis solutions, however, do not produce unique factor scores; the principal components method does (Kim and Mueller, 1978; Rummel, 1970).

47. Pronouns and ambiguous references were identified in the text.

48. These definitions are from Stone et al. (1966: 174-176). The remaining definitions are from Namenwirth (no date).

49. ANOVA is used in the analysis of categorical independent and continuous dependent variables (e.g., see Rosenthal and Rosnow, 1984).

50. There were three time periods corresponding to June 25, 1950, to October 31, 1950 (the beginning of hostilities until the intervention of the Chinese); November 1, 1950, to July 7, 1951 (the Chinese intervention until the beginning of truce talks); and July 8, 1951, to August 11, 1953 (the onset of truce talks until 15 days after signing the truce agreement).

51. The principal components method was used, which, as noted, excludes unique variances but retains common and error variances (Kim and Mueller, 1978; Rummel, 1970).

52. One can calculate the reliability of factor scores obtained through principal components by calculating the Theta reliability coefficient (Armor, 1974).

53. This research was conducted by Hans-Dieter Klingemann at Freie Universitat Berlin, Peter Philip Mohler, and the present writer.

54. The idea of acceleration or changes in the rate of change may not be intuitively obvious, and so a few examples may help to clarify the matter. For each year the acceleration (or deceleration) of the economy is derived from prices for three years. If wheat prices are 50, 65, and 55 marks per ton in 1871, 1872, and 1873 respectively, then for 1872 and 1873 the first differences are 15 and –10 respectively. The second difference for 1873 is –25 (–10 – 15). Hence concern with wealth in 1873 is likely to be somewhat higher than average. This is intuitively plausible because the economy was improving between 1871 and 1872 and declining between 1872 and 1873. Consider another series of prices: 50, 55, and 65. Here the first differences are 5 and 10, and the second difference is 5. This would show that the economy is growing at an increasing rate of change, and hence one would expect that in the third year the level of wealth concerns would be lower than average.

55. Figure 3.3 presents the values of various coefficients and the symbols frequently used to represent them in LISREL models. These are (see Jöreskog and Sörbom, 1979, and Long, 1983a, 1983b, for a technical discussion and more detailed explication):

1. Lambda Y (LY): factor loadings of the observed Y's on the unobserved dependent variables;
2. Lambda X (LX): factor loadings of the observed X's on the unobserved independent variables;
3. Theta Delta (TD): covariance matrix of the residuals or error term for the measurement model of the latent independent variables;

4. Theta Epsilon (TE): covariance matrix of the residuals or error term for the measurement model of the latent dependent variables;
5. Beta (BE): causal coefficients among the dependent variables;
6. Gamma (GA): causal coefficients linking dependent and independent variables;
7. Phi (PH): covariance matrix of the latent independent variables; and,
8. Psi (PS): covariance matrix of the residuals in the structured model.

56. Using the data reported above, however, Jan-Bernd Lohmoller and Herman Wold (1984) estimated our model using two alternative procedures, canonical correlation and partial least-squares "soft modeling" (Wold, 1975, 1981). Using procedures that make weaker statistical assumptions, they found weaker relationships between economic performance and wealth concerns. I believe, however, that the stronger assumptions incorporated in the LISREL model are justifiable. In any event, this research is still in the exploratory phase and — irrespective of estimation technique — the hypothesized negative relationship between economic performance and wealth concerns is confirmed.

57. Chapter 3 shows that these measures are, in turn, sometimes analyzed using statistical techniques such as factor analysis to generate indicators of themes, issues, and dilemmas. Namenwirth and Weber (1987: chapter 8) address problems resulting from different measurement models for indicators of themes.

58. Another form of categorical equivalence is *denotative categorical equivalence*. Textual units are denotative categorically equivalent if they have the same meaning, such as *purchase* and *buy*.

59. When words take on new meanings, the disambiguation procedures noted earlier generally handle large differences of meaning; the discussion here concerns less obvious differences.

60. In some content analysis research (e.g., Namenwirth and Weber, 1987), referents of pronouns and other anaphoras were edited manually into the text.

61. There is nothing inherent in the text classification procedures described above that requires the unit of analysis to be the entire document. Other units can be used, such as paragraphs or sentences. In related research, Saris-Gallhofer and her colleagues (1978) found that shorter coding units, such as words, yielded higher validity than longer coding units such as sentences, paragraphs, or entire texts. An area for future research, however, is the consequences for validity and reliability of aggregating word counts at various levels, such as sentences or paragraphs.

62. UNDERSTATE and OVERSTATE are categories from the Harvard dictionary (Dunphy et al., 1989; Stone et al., 1966; Zuell et al., 1989). OVERSTATE contains words providing emphasis in the following areas: speed, frequency, inevitability, causality, inclusiveness of persons, objects, or places, quantity in numerical and quasi-numerical terms, accuracy and validity, importance, intensity, likelihood, certainty, and extremity. UNDERSTATE contains words providing de-emphasis in the following areas: speed, frequency, inevitability, causality, inclusiveness of persons, objects or places, quantity in numerical and quasi-numerical terms, accuracy and validity, importance, scope, size, clarity, exceptionalness, intensity, likelihood, certainty, and extremity (i.e., emphasizing slowness rather than speed, infrequency rather than frequency; Dunphy et al., 1989).

63. This kind of primitive disambiguation is only a modest step. Chief among its practical advantages is that it relies on inexpensive technology. Computers can process large amounts of text quickly at nominal cost.

64. The results of the computer-aided classification and statistical procedures suggested both the duration and interpretation of this thematic cycle. The following excerpts span 67 years, which is close enough to the 72-year average cycle.

65. "Class conflict" is probably not appropriate here because industrial capitalism had yet to appear and the country was firmly in the grips of mercantilist theories and practices.

66. The integrative issue is itself interpreted as part of a four-phase problem-solving sequence posited by Bales (1950, 1953; Bales and Strodtbeck, 1953) and Parsons (Parsons and Bales, 1953; Parsons, Bales, and Shils, 1953; see Parsons and Smelser, 1956) the purpose of which is the pursuit of system rather than subgroup (e.g., class) goals.

REFERENCES

AGER, D. E., KNOWLES, F. E., and SMITH, J. (1979) Advances in Computer-Aided Literary and Linguistic Research. University of Aston, Birmingham, England: Department of Modern Languages.

AITKEN, A. J., BAILEY, R. W., and HAMILTON-SMITH, N. (eds.) (1973) The Computer and Literary Studies. Edinburgh: Edinburgh University Press.

ALLEN, J. (1987) Natural Language Understanding. Menlo Park, CA: Benjamin/Cummings.

ALTHAUSER, R. P. (1974) "Inferring validity from the multitrait-multimethod matrix: Another assessment," in H. L. Costner (ed.) Sociological Methodology 1973-1974. San Francisco: Jossey-Bass.

ALWIN, D. F. (1974) "Approaches to the interpretation of relationships in the multitrait-multimethod matrix," in H. L. Costner (ed.) Sociological Methodology 1973-1974. San Francisco: Jossey-Bass.

ANDERSON, A. B. (1970) "Structure of semantic space," in E. F. Borgatta (ed.) Sociological Methodology 1970. San Francisco: Jossey-Bass.

ARIES, E. (1973) Interaction Patterns and Themes of Male, Female, and Mixed Groups. Unpublished Ph.D. dissertation, Harvard University.

ARIES, E. (1977) "Male-female interpersonal styles in all male, all female, and mixed groups," in A. G. Sargent (ed.) Beyond Sex Roles. St. Paul: West.

ARMOR, D. J. (1974) "Theta reliability and factor scaling," in H. L. Costner (ed.) Sociological Methodology 1973-1974. San Francisco: Jossey-Bass.

AXELROD, R. (ed.) (1976) Structure of Decision: The Cognitive Maps of Political Elites. Princeton: Princeton University Press.

Ayer Directory of Publications. (1983) Philadelphia: Ayer.

BALES, R. F. (1950) Interaction Process Analysis: A Method for the Study of Small Groups. Reading, MA: Addison-Wesley.

BALES, R. F. (1953) "The equilibrium problem in small groups," pp. 111-161 in T. Parsons, R. F. Bales, and E. Shils (eds.) Working Papers in the Theory of Action. New York: Free Press.

BALES, R. F. and STRODTBECK, F. L. (1953) "Phases in group problem solving." Journal of Abnormal and Social Psychology 46: 485-495.

BERELSON, B. (1952) Content Analysis in Communications Research. New York: Free Press.

BERRY-ROGGHE, G. L. M. (1973) "Computation of collocations in lexical studies," in A. J. Aitken, R. W. Bailey, and N. Hamilton-Smith (eds.) The Computer and Literary Studies. Edinburgh: Edinburgh University Press.

BLALOCK, H. M. (ed.) (1974) Measurement in the Social Sciences. Chicago: Aldine.

BODEN, M. (1987) Artificial Intelligence and Natural Man (2nd ed.). New York: Basic Books.

BODEN, M. (1988) Computer Models of Mind. Cambridge: Cambridge University Press.

BRADY, M. and BERWICK, R. C. (eds.) (1983) Computational Models of Discourse. Cambridge: MIT Press.

BRENT, E. (1984) "Qualitative computing: Approaches and issues." Qualitative Sociology 7(1/2).

BRINBERG, D. and KIDDER, L. H. (eds.) (1982) Forms of Validity in Research. San Francisco: Jossey-Bass.

BRINBERG, D. and MCGRATH, J. E. (1982) "A network of validity concepts within the research process," in D. Brinberg and L. H. Kidder (eds.) Forms of Validity in Research. San Francisco: Jossey-Bass.

BRINBERG, D. and MCGRATH, J. E. (1985) Validity and the Research Process. Beverly Hills, CA: Sage.

BRUNNER, R. D. (1983) Forecasting Growth Ideologies. Discussion paper no. 7. Boulder: University of Colorado Center for Public Policy Research.

BRUNNER, R. D. (1984) The President's Annual Message. Discussion paper no. 8. Boulder: University of Colorado Center for Public Policy Research.

BRUNNER, R. D. and LIVORNESE, K. (1982) Subjective Political Change: A Prospectus. Discussion paper no. 5. Boulder: University of Colorado Center for Public Policy Research.

BUDGE, I., ROBERTSON, D., and HEARL, D. (eds.) (1987) Ideology, Strategy and Party Change: Spatial Analyses of Post-War Election Programmes in 19 Democracies. Cambridge: Cambridge University Press.

BURNHAM, W. D. (1970) Critical Elections and the Mainsprings of American Politics. New York: Norton.

BURTON, D. M. (1981) "Automated concordances and word indexes: The process, the programs, and the products." Computers and the Humanities 15: 139-154.

BURTON, D. M. (1982) "Automated concordances and word-indexes: Machine decisions and editorial revisions." Computers and the Humanities 16: 195-218.

CAMPBELL, D. T. and FISKE, D. W. (1959) "Convergent and discriminant validation by the multitrait-multimethod matrix." Psychological Bulletin 56: 81-105.

CAMPBELL, D. T. and O'CONNELL, E. J. (1982) "Methods as diluting trait relationships rather than adding irrelevant systematic variance," in D. Brinberg and L. H. Kidder (eds.) Forms of Validity in Research. San Francisco: Jossey-Bass.

CAMPBELL, D. T. and STANLEY, J. C. (1963) Experimental and Quasi-Experimental Designs for Research. Chicago: Rand McNally.

CARBONELL, J. G. (1981) Subjective Understanding: Computer Models of Belief Systems. Ann Arbor: UMI Research Press.

CARMINES, E. G. and ZELLER, R. A. (1982) Reliability and Validity Assessment. Beverly Hills, CA: Sage.

CLEVELAND, C., MCTAVISH, D., and PIRRO, E. (1974) Quester-Contextual Content Analysis Methodology. Paper presented at 1974 Pisa Conference on Content Analysis.

COOK, T. D. and CAMPBELL, D. T. (1979) Quasi-Experimentation: Design & Analysis for Field Settings. Chicago: Rand McNally.

CRONBACH, L. J. and MEEHL, P. E. (1955) "Construct validity in psychological tests." Psychological Bulletin 52: 281-302.

DEWEESE, L. C., III. (1976) "Computer content analysis of printed media: A limited feasibility study." Public Opinion Quarterly 40: 92-100.

DEWEESE, L. C., III. (1977) "Computer content analysis of 'day-old' newspapers: A feasibility study." Public Opinion Quarterly 41: 91-94.

DUNPHY, D. C., BULLARD, C. G., and CROSSING, E. E. M. (1974) "Validation of the General Inquirer Harvard IV Dictionary." Paper presented at the 1974 Pisa Conference on Content Analysis.

DUNPHY, D. C., BULLARD, C. G., and CROSSING, E. E. M. (1989) "Validation of the General Inquirer Harvard IV Dictionary," in C. Zuell, R. P. Weber, and P. Mohler,

Computer-assisted Text Analysis for the Social Sciences: The General Inquirer III. Mannheim, FRG: Center for Surveys, Methods, and Analysis (ZUMA).

DYER, M. G. (1983) In-Depth Understanding: A Computer Model of Integrated Processing of Narrative Comprehension. Cambridge: MIT Press.

FIRTH, J. R. (1957) "Modes of meaning," in Papers in Linguistics 1934-51. London: Oxford University Press.

FISKE, D. W. (1982) "Convergent-discriminant validation in measurements and research strategies," pp. 72-92 in D. Brinberg and L. H. Kidder (eds.) Forms of Validation in Research. San Francisco: Jossey-Bass.

FREEMAN, M. F. and TUKEY, J. W. (1950) "Transformation related to the angular and the square root." Annals of Mathematical Statistics 21: 607-611.

GEFFROY, A., LAFON, P., SEIDEL, G., and TOURNIER, M. (1973) "Lexicometric analysis of co-occurrences," in A. J. Aitken, R. W. Bailey, and N. Hamilton-Smith (eds.) The Computer and Literary Studies. Edinburgh: Edinburgh University Press.

GEORGE, A. L. (1959a) Propaganda Analysis. Evanston: Row, Peterson.

GEORGE, A. L. (1959b) "Quantitative and qualitative approaches to content analysis," in I. D. S. Pool (ed.) Trends in Content Analysis. Urbana: University of Illinois Press.

GERBNER, G., HOLSTI, O. R., KRIPPENDORFF, K., PAISLEY, W., and STONE, P. J. (eds.) (1969) The Analysis of Communication Content. New York: John Wiley.

GOTTSCHALK, L. A. (1979) The Content Analysis of Verbal Behavior: Further Studies. New York: SP Medical & Scientific Books.

GOTTSCHALK, L. A., LOLAS, F., and VINEX, L. L. (eds.) (1986) Content Analysis of Verbal Behavior. New York/Berlin: Springer-Verlag.

GREY, A., KAPLAN, D., and LASSWELL, H. D. (1965) "Recording and context units—four ways of coding editorial content," in H. D. Lasswell, N. Leites, and Associates (eds.) Language of Politics. Cambridge: MIT Press.

HASKEL, P. J. (1971) "Collocations as a measure of stylistic variety," in R. A. Wisbey (ed.) The Computer in Literary and Linguistic Research. Cambridge: Cambridge University Press.

HERZOG, A. (1973) The BS Factor. New York: Simon & Schuster.

HOCKEY, S. and MARRIOTT, I. (1982) Oxford Concordance Program Version 1.0 Users' Manual. Oxford: Oxford University Computing Service.

HOCKEY, S. and MARTIN, J. (1987) "The Oxford Concordance program version 2." Literary and Linguistic Computing 2: 125-131.

HOLSTI, O. R. (1963) "Computer content analysis," in R. C. North, O. R. Holsti, M. G. Zaninovich, and D. A. Zinnes, Content Analysis: A Handbook with Applications for the Study of International Crises. Evanston: Northwestern University Press.

HOLSTI, O. R. (1966) "External conflict and internal consensus: The Sino-Soviet case," in P. J. Stone et al., The General Inquirer: A Computer Approach to Content Analysis. Cambridge: MIT Press.

HOLSTI, O. R. (1969) Content Analysis for the Social Sciences and Humanities. Reading, MA: Addison-Wesley.

IKER, H. P. (1965) "A computer approach toward the analysis of content." Behavioral Science 10: 173-183.

IKER, H. P. (1974) "An historical note on the use of word-frequency contiguities in content analysis." Computers and the Humanities 8: 93-98.

92

IKER, H. P. and HARWAY, N. I. (1969) "A computer systems approach to the recognition and analysis of content," in G. Gerbner et al. (eds.) The Analysis of Communication Content. New York: John Wiley.

JANIS, I. L. (1965) "The problem of validating content analysis," in H. D. Lasswell, N. Leites, and Associates (eds.) Language of Politics. Cambridge: MIT Press.

JOHNSON, D. B. (1979) National Party Platforms 1840-1976 (2 vols.). Urbana: University of Illinois Press.

JOHNSON, D. B. (1982) National Party Platforms of 1980. Urbana: University of Illinois Press.

JONES, A. and CHURCHHOUSE, R. F. (eds.) (1976) The Computer in Literary and Linguistic Studies. Cardiff: University of Wales Press.

JÖRESKOG, K. G. and SÖRBOM, D. (1979) Advances in Factor Analysis and Structural Equation Models. Cambridge, MA: Abt.

JÖRESKOG, K. G. and SÖRBOM, D. (1984) LISREL VI (Analysis of Linear Structural Relationships by the Method of Maximum Likelihood) Users Guide. Mooresville, IN: Scientific Software, Inc.

KELLY, E. F. and STONE, P. J. (1975) Computer Recognition of English Word Senses. Amsterdam: North Holland.

KIM, J. -O. and MUELLER, C. W. (1978) Factor Analysis: Statistical Methods and Practical Issues. Beverly Hills, CA: Sage.

KLINGEMANN, H. D., MOHLER, R. P., and WEBER, R. P. (1982) "Cultural indicators based on content analysis." Quality and Quantity 16: 1-18.

KRIPPENDORFF, K. (1980) Content Analysis: An Introduction to Its Methodology. Beverly Hills, CA: Sage.

LASSWELL, H. D. and KAPLAN, A. (1950) Power and Society: A Framework for Political Inquiry. New Haven: Yale University Press.

LASSWELL, H. D., LEITES, N., and Associates (eds.) (1965) Language of Politics. Cambridge: MIT Press.

LASSWELL, H. D., LERNER, D., and POOL, I. D. S. (1952) The Comparative Study of Symbols. Stanford: Stanford University Press.

LEHMAN, E. W. (1977) Political Society: A Macrosociology of Politics. New York: Columbia University Press.

LOHMOLLER, J. -B. and WOLD, H. (1984) "Introduction to PLS estimation of path models with latent variables including some recent developments on mixed scale variables," in G. Melischek, K. E. Rosengren, and J. Stappers (eds.) Cultural Indicators: An International Symposium. Vienna: Austrian Academy of Sciences.

LONG, J. S. (1983a) Confirmatory Factor Analysis: A Preface to LISREL. Beverly Hills, CA: Sage.

LONG, J. S. (1983b) Covariance Structure Models: An Introduction to LISREL. Beverly Hills, CA: Sage.

LORD, F. M. and NOVICK, M. R. (1968) The Statistical Analysis of Mental Test Scores. Reading, MA: Addison-Wesley.

MARKOFF, J., SHAPIRO, G., and WEITMAN, S. (1974) "Toward the integration of content analysis and general methodology," in D. R. Heise (ed.) Sociological Methodology, 1975. San Francisco: Jossey-Bass.

MELISCHEK, G., ROSENGREN, K. E., and STAPPERS, J. (eds.) (1984) Cultural Indicators: An International Symposium. Vienna: Austrian Academy of Sciences.

MERRIAM, J. E. and MAKOWER, J. (1988) Trend Watching: How the Media Create Trends and How to be the First to Uncover Them. New York: American Management Association.

MERRITT, R. L. (1966) Symbols of American Community 1735-1775. New Haven: Yale University Press.

MOSTELLER, F. and WALLACE, D. L. (1964) Inference and Disputed Authorship: The Federalist. Reading, MA: Addison-Wesley.

NAISBITT, J. (1982) Megatrends. New York: Warner Books.

NAMENWIRTH, J. Z. (no date) The Namenwirth Political Dictionary. Unpublished manuscript.

NAMENWIRTH, J. Z. (1969a) "Marks of distinction: A content analysis of British mass and prestige newspaper editorials." American Journal of Sociology 74: 343-360.

NAMENWIRTH, J. Z. (1969b) "Some long and short term trends in one American political value," in G. Gerbner et al., The Analysis of Communication Content. New York: John Wiley.

NAMENWIRTH, J. Z. (1970) "Prestige newspapers and the assessment of elite opinions." Journalism Quarterly 47: 318-323.

NAMENWIRTH, J. Z. (1973) "The wheels of time and the interdependence of value change." Journal of Interdisciplinary History 3: 649-683.

NAMENWIRTH, J. Z. (1984a) "Why cultural indicators?" in G. Melischek, K. E. Rosengren, and J. Stappers (eds.) Cultural Indicators. Vienna: Austrian Academy of Sciences.

NAMENWIRTH, J. Z. and BIBBEE, R. (1975) "Speech codes in the press." Journal of Communication 25: 50-63.

NAMENWIRTH, J. Z. and LASSWELL, H. D. (1970) The Changing Language of American Values: A Computer Study of Selected Party Platforms. Beverly Hills, CA: Sage.

NAMENWIRTH, J. Z. and WEBER, R. P. (1987) Dynamics of Culture. Winchester, MA: Allen & Unwin.

NORTH, R. C., HOLSTI, O. R., ZANINOVICH, M. G., and ZINNES, D. A. (1963) Content Analysis: A Handbook with Applications for the Study of International Crises. Evanston: Northwestern University Press.

OAKMAN, R. L. (1980) Computer Methods for Literary Research. Columbia: University of South Carolina Press.

OGILVIE, D. M. (1966) "Procedures for improving the interpretation of tag scores: The case of Windle," in P. J. Stone et al., The General Inquirer: A Computer Approach to Content Analysis. Cambridge: MIT Press.

OGILVIE, D. M., STONE, P. J., and KELLY, E. F. (1980) "Computer-aided content analysis," in R. B. Smith and P. K. Manning (eds.) Handbook of Social Science Research Methods. New York: Irvington.

OGILVIE, D. M., STONE, P. J., and SHNEIDMAN, E. S. (1966) "Some characteristics of genuine versus simulated suicide notes," in P. J. Stone et al., The General Inquirer: A Computer Approach to Content Analysis. Cambridge: MIT Press.

ORWELL, G. (1949) Nineteen Eighty-Four, A Novel. New York: Harcourt Brace.

OSGOOD, C. E., MAY, W. H., and MIRON, M. S. (1975) Cross-Cultural Universals of Affective Meaning. Urbana: University of Illinois Press.

OSGOOD, C. E., SUCI, G. J., and TANNENBAUM, P. H. (1957) The Measurement of Meaning. Urbana: University of Illinois Press.

PARSONS, T. (1969) "On the concept of political power," in T. Parsons, Politics and Social Structure. New York: Free Press.

PARSONS, T. and BALES, R. F. (1953) "The dimensions of action-space," pp. 63-109 in T. Parsons, R. F. Bales, and E. A. Shils (eds.) Working Papers in the Theory of Action. New York: Free Press.

PARSONS, T., BALES, R. F., and SHILS, E. A. (1953) "Phase movement in relation to motivation, symbol formation, and role structure," pp. 163-268 in T. Parsons, R. F. Bales, and E. A. Shils (eds.) Working Papers in the Theory of Action. New York: Free Press.

PARSONS, T. and SMELSER, N. (1956) Economy and Society. New York: Free Press.

POOL, I. D. S. (1951) Symbols of Internationalism. Stanford: Stanford University Press.

POOL, I. D. S. (1952a) The "Prestige Papers": A Survey of Their Editorials. Stanford: Stanford University Press.

POOL, I. D. S. (1952b) Symbols of Democracy. Stanford: Stanford University Press.

POOL, I. D. S. (ed.) (1959) Trends in Content Analysis. Urbana: University of Illinois Press.

PRESTON, M. J. and COLEMAN, S. S. (1978) "Some considerations concerning encoding and concording texts." Computers and the Humanities 12: 3-12.

ROSENGREN, K. E. (ed.) (1981) Advances in Content Analysis. Beverly Hills, CA: Sage.

ROSENTHAL, R. (1984) Meta-Analytic Procedures for Social Research. Beverly Hills, CA: Sage.

ROSENTHAL, R. and ROSNOW, R. L. (1984) Essentials of Behavioral Research: Methods and Data Analysis. New York: McGraw-Hill.

RUMMEL, R. J. (1970) Applied Factor Analysis. Evanston: Northwestern University Press.

SALTON, G. (1989) Automatic Test Processing. Reading, MA: Addison-Wesley.

SARIS-GALLHOFER, I. N., SARIS, W. E., and MORTON, E. L. (1978) "A validation study of Holsti's content analysis procedure." Quality and Quantity 12: 131-145.

SCHANK, R. C. and ABELSON, R. P. (1977) Scripts, Plans, Goals, and Understanding. Hillsdale, NJ: Lawrence Erlbaum.

SCHUESSLER, K. (1970) Analyzing Social Data: A Statistical Orientation. Boston: Houghton Mifflin.

SLATER, P. (1966) Microcosm. New York: John Wiley.

SMITH, R. G. (1978) The Message Measurement Inventory: A Profile for Communication Analysis. Bloomington: Indiana University Press.

SNIDER, J. G. and OSGOOD, C. E. (eds.) (1969) Semantic Differential Technique: A Sourcebook. Chicago: Aldine.

STEFFLRE, V. (1965) "Simulation of people's behavior toward new objects and events." American Behavioral Scientist 8: 12-15.

STEINER, G. (1975) After Babel: Aspects of Language and Translation. Oxford: Oxford University Press.

STONE, P. J., DUNPHY, D. C., SMITH, M. S., and OGILVIE, D. M. (1966) The General Inquirer: A Computer Approach to Content Analysis. Cambridge: MIT Press.

TUFTE, E. R. (1978) Political Control of the Economy. Princeton: Princeton University Press.

WALKER, A. W. (1975) The Empirical Delineation of Two Musical Taste Cultures: A Content Analysis of Best-Selling Soul and Popular Recordings from 1962-1973. Unpublished Ph.D. dissertation, New School for Social Research.

WEBB, E. J., CAMPBELL, D. T., SCHWARTZ, R. D., and SECHRIST, L. (1981) Nonreactive Measures in the Social Sciences. Boston: Houghton Mifflin.

WEBER, R. P. (1981) "Society and economy in the Western world system." Social Forces 59: 1130-1148.

WEBER, R. P. (1982) "The long-term problem-solving dynamics of social systems." European Journal of Political Research 10: 387-405.

WEBER, R. P. (1983) "Measurement models for content analysis." Quality and Quantity 17: 127-149.

WEBER, R. P. (1984a) "Content analytic cultural indicators," in G. Melischek, K. E. Rosengren, and J. Stappers (eds.) Cultural Indicators: An International Symposium. Vienna: Austrian Academy of Sciences.

WEBER, R. P. (1984b) "Content analysis: A short primer." Qualitative Sociology 7: 126-147.

WEBER, R. P. and NAMENWIRTH, J. Z. (in press) "Content analytic culture indicators: A self-critique," in Advances in Computing and the Humanities (vol. 3). Greenwich, CT: JAI.

WEIZENBAUM, J. (1976) Computer Power and Human Reason. San Francisco: Freeman.

WILLIAMS, R. (1985) Keywords: A Vocabulary of Culture and Society (rev. ed.). New York: Oxford University Press.

WINOGRAD, T. (1983) Language As a Cognitive Process, Volume 1. Syntax. Reading, MA: Addison-Wesley.

WINOGRAD, T. and FLORES, F. (1986) Understanding Computers and Cognition: A New Foundation for Design. Norwood, NJ: Ablex.

WISBEY, R. A. (1971) The Computer in Literary and Linguistic Research. Cambridge: Cambridge University Press.

WOLD, H. (1975) "Soft modelling by latent variables: The non-linear iterative partial least squares (NIPALS) approach," in J. Gani (ed.) Perspectives in Probability and Statistics, Papers in Honour of M. S. Bartlett. London: Academic Press.

WOLD, H. (1981) "Model construction and evaluation when theoretical knowledge is scarce: On the theory and application of partial least squares," in J. Kmenta and J. Ramsey (eds.) Evaluation of Econometric Models. New York: Academic Press.

ZELLER, R. A. and CARMINES, E. G. (1980) Measurement in the Social Sciences. Cambridge: Cambridge University Press.

ZIPF, G. K. (1932) Selected Studies of the Principle of Relative Frequency in Language. Cambridge, MA: Harvard University Press.

ZIPF, G. K. (1965) Psycho-biology of Language. Cambridge: MIT Press.

ZUELL, C., WEBER, R. P., and MOHLER, P. P. (1989) Computer-assisted Text Analysis for the Social Sciences: The General Inquirer III. Mannheim, FRG: Center for Surveys, Methods, and Analysis (ZUMA).

ABOUT THE AUTHOR

ROBERT PHILIP WEBER (Ph.D., Sociology) is currently a Principal of Northeast Consulting Resources, Inc., a Boston consulting firm. He is a founding member of the Sociology of Culture section of the American Sociological Association and past editor of *Culture,* the section newsletter. He has been a Fullbright fellow and guest professor and lecturer in Germany, Sweden, the Netherlands, and the United Kingdom. The author of more than a dozen papers on content analysis and on long-term social, economic, political, and cultural change, he is also co-author with J. Z. Namenwirth of *Dynamics of Culture* (1987) and co-author with C. Zuell and P. Ph. Mohler of *Computer-Assisted Text Analysis for the Social Sciences: The General Inquirer III* (1989). With P. J. Stone, he is co-author of the article on "content analysis" in the *Encyclopedia of Sociology* (1992).